AWAKENINGS

First published in Great Britain in 2020 Sphere

1 3 5 7 9 10 8 6 4 2

A CIP catalogue record for this book
is available from the British Library.

ISBN 978-0-7515-8060-0

Editorial Director: Rhiannon Smith
Commissioning Editor: Fiona Rose
Photographer: Joanna Bongard
Props Stylist: Felicity Landrock-Mettam
Production Manager: Abby Marshall
Cover Design: Sophie Harris

Typeset in FreightBig Pro and Sofia Pro
Printed and bound at Mohn Media, Germany
Papers used by Sphere are from well-managed forests
and other responsible sources.

Sphere
An imprint of
Little, Brown Book Group
Carmelite House
50 Victoria Embankment
London EC4Y 0DZ
An Hachette UK Company

www.hachette.co.uk

www.littlebrown.co.uk

lucy watson

AWAKENINGS

A Guide to Living a Vegan Lifestyle

sphere

Contents

Introduction

I f you'd asked me ten years ago if I ever saw myself going vegan, I would probably have laughed and said, 'Never in a million years. I care about animals, but vegans are just a bit extreme.'

At that point in my life, I was a pescatarian (someone who eats fish but not meat) who loved cheese and managed to eat it nearly every single meal of the day. I also wore things like leather and wool without much of a second thought. But I still thought of myself as living a mindful and cruelty-free life. Having grown up on a farm and acquired a better insight than most as to what actually goes on in rearing livestock, I knew eating meat wasn't something I wanted to be a part of. No living thing needed to suffer for me to enjoy a meal and that was the end of it.

At the time, I thought that was enough. I thought I was fully conscious of animal welfare, especially in contrast to friends of mine who loved feasting on sausages and beef burgers. I was anti-fur and anti-animal testing, but I didn't see how illogical it was to be anti-fur and yet wear leather, for example. I believed leather to be a by-product of the meat industry and by not eating meat I thought I was solving my contribution to that issue.

At this point, I thought I was awake, but I was living a life with my eyes closed.

This book is called *Awakenings* in tribute to this process of consciously understanding what it truly means to live a cruelty-free, animal-loving life. Awakening to the way in which animals are exploited for our benefit can be a hard emotional journey, especially once you realise the extent to which animal cruelty has infiltrated the products we consume every day. It can feel overwhelming and upsetting – I have spent hours crying at some of the things I've seen. But all change starts with education: that's what gives you the motivation to start living differently.

I want everyone who reads this book to come away reassured that there are vegan solutions to pretty much any issue you can think of. I don't want anyone to feel that they are alone in looking for answers, or that it's impossible to find a vegan alternative, because there will be a way.

Yes, you can still have pizza. Yes, you can still wear beautiful and cool clothes. Yes, you can still eat out. Yes, you can still pamper yourself with beauty products that are just as good as (if not better than) the ones you may have been using before. And when you are doing this in the knowl-

"

**All change starts
with education:
that's what gives you
the motivation to start
living differently.**

"

edge that your actions are not hurting animals, I promise, everything will taste and feel so much better. It will feel *right*.

See, being vegan doesn't just mean changing the way you eat. That's obviously where most people start, but there is so much more to *living* vegan than you may first anticipate. I want to share my vegan journey with you, to inspire you to make changes of your own, and share the knowledge and lessons I have learned along the way.

Get ready to be awakened . . .

What is Veganism?

The Vegan Society defines veganism as:

> *A way of living which seeks to exclude, as far as is possible and practicable, all forms of exploitation of, and cruelty to, animals for food, clothing or any other purpose.*[1]

Although diets that exclude animal products have a long and ancient history, the word 'vegan' was created in 1944, by a British woodworker named Donald Watson (no relation). Because vegetarians ate dairy and eggs, he wanted a term to describe people who did not. (Rejected words included 'dairyban', 'vitan', and 'benevore'.) By the time Watson died at the age of ninety-five in 2005, there were 250,000 vegans in Britain and two million in the USA – and the numbers have kept on growing.[2]

Here's how I define it, personally: a vegan is someone who avoids eating animal products, which for me means meat, fish, eggs, dairy and honey. Some argue that it goes deeper than that – for example, that avocados aren't vegan because they are grown using bees in the pollination process – and it all starts to get quite complicated. But for me personally, in terms of diet, it comes down to avoiding those five products. You don't have to follow the way that I do it, but this is what I feel comfortable with.

" There is no such thing as the perfect vegan. "

For me, being vegan is also about making a *conscious effort* to avoid animal products in all areas of your life – in clothing, around the home, and even by thinking carefully about what attractions you visit on holiday. The notion of consciousness is really important to me in how I think of veganism: it's about constantly educating yourself, becoming more aware and looking for the truth.

I know that even as I write this book there may be things that I do in my current life that harm others that I am not completely aware of. But that's OK, I'm open to that fact and know that when the information comes to my attention I will be ready to adjust (or think about adjusting) my lifestyle to suit. Nothing shocks me any more.

It's also about effort. I am very aware that everyone has a different life, a different level of income and different options available to them. Everyone's vegan journey will accordingly, be different, but what matters is that you keep trying, and keep putting effort in to live a vegan lifestyle. You will rarely meet two vegans who have exactly the same views on everything because there really is so much ground to cover. But one thing you will know is that they are *trying* to do better and that is usually something we can bond over.

There is no such thing as the perfect vegan. Where do you draw a line? For example, paper money contains animal product (very unnecessary but who's surprised here?). But until this changes, there are certain situations which make it hard to avoid handling money. Veganism as a lifestyle can get quite complicated but I come back to this principle of making a conscious effort to avoid animal products in all areas of your life, and I find it a good guide.

I will add that I am also very against an animal being used as a commodity – making money out of them isn't right. They don't have a choice in the matter and a lot of the time it can result in unpleasant experiences for them purely for someone else to profit. I've also found this a good guideline to follow if I am unsure of whether something is right or wrong.

Now that I am vegan, I feel that I am authentically being myself. It feels like this is how I was meant to be, without the fog of confusion that has sent me in other directions in my life: school, family influence, marketing. It doesn't feel like an effort; it feels natural to live like this. That's not to say it doesn't sometimes *require* effort – a vegan lifestyle can sometimes require more research, and this is very much the case when brands hide stuff, don't label things correctly, and are so keen to put out a misinforming image compared to the reality.

But I know it's always worth it. Living as a vegan, I feel like the real me. I feel I can truly call myself an animal lover.

"

Living as a vegan, I feel
like the real me.
I feel I can truly call myself
an animal lover.

"

My Journey

I want to share my vegan journey with you to show you the moments of awakening that really changed the way I view the world. I hope some of these will help you see things differently too.

I also want to share it to show that becoming vegan wasn't an overnight thing – I didn't wake up one morning and find myself the perfect vegan. Everyone's journey will be different and that's OK.

As you will see from my own experiences, changes came at different times, as I learned more and more along the way. Sometimes I resisted a change, believing that I knew best, or that I already knew the reality of what was going on. Or – and it's important to be honest – sometimes it was because I didn't *want* to know what was going on. I often had a gut instinct that I should look further into an issue, but sometimes ignored that because it was just easier to keep going as I was. Sometimes I would feel slightly overwhelmed with all that I did know; that I really wasn't ready to discover more.

What was and is important to me is that I commit to educating myself and keep pushing on. It's very likely that you will stumble along the way. What matters is getting yourself back on the path afterwards.

All about the animals

From as far back as I can remember, I have always loved animals. They are so easy to be around and give us so much, while demanding so little. I've always felt they are a safe space – there's no judgement from them. They're just straightforward, and so incredibly loyal. I also love how each individual creature is unique. Each one has their own personality – and this is something we are taught to ignore in our consumption of them, to see them just as commodities and not as individual beings. But when you start to notice the individual traits of an animal, it's such a joyful thing getting to know them. Each has their own personality and they don't try to be anything else – they're purely themselves.

When we were growing up, we always had pets – dogs, cats and even budgies. My mum is a huge animal lover, and was a role model in how to interact with animals. She was always so loving and caring to them, and that really showed me and my sister how to be compassionate as well.

When I was about five or six, we moved to a farm. The thinking was that for animal lovers, it would be a wonderful place to grow up. But at this point, as a young child, I didn't realise that a farm was a place where animals are raised for slaughter. There is such a disconnect between the idyllic image of a farm that we give to children when we encourage them to play with farm sets, or even visit petting farms to interact with the animals, and the reality of what farming really is. At that age, you just believe what you are told by the society around you, and these influences come from everywhere – from your parents to your school to what you might see on TV.

"

Sometimes I resisted a change, believing that I knew best, or that I already knew the reality of what was going on.

"

But there were things at the farm that always seemed off. I remember when we went to look round, we saw a strange room (now converted into a gym) – there was blood on the floor and knives on the wall. I was instinctively horrified and afraid, but I didn't know what this room was for. I didn't ask questions; I was only five at the time. I didn't know how to make sense of what I'd seen, as I was so young, but the memory lingered with me.

Once we were living on the farm, I was aware of the high turnover of animals. The trucks that pulled up, the way the animals were loaded on, how they were crying and bleating, how they would try and get back out – it was really quite traumatic to witness, let alone for them to experience.

On the farm, we had cows, sheep, lambs and chickens. We were very hands-on, helping with the lambing and bottle feeding the baby lambs as necessary, and of course we loved and bonded with the animals. Each one had their own little personality and quirks. I'll also add that we ate meat every day. Somehow, though, the meat on my plate just didn't seem connected with the animals we were caring for every day. The ones that ran over to us in the field and enjoyed cuddles and strokes from us. They trusted us. Were they wrong to do this? Yes. Did they have any clue what their lives would amount to and who would be in control of how it ended? No.

The first major awakening in my life was the day when I came home from school and my pet lamb, Maisy, who I'd been bottle-feeding and who we'd raised as a family, was gone. Suddenly, I added up everything I had seen. The dots were joined at last and the horrible picture was revealed. I realised she hadn't just *gone*, she had gone to be killed, for meat, along with all her lamb friends. She was dead. From that moment on, I decided I would never eat meat again.

My family's response was quite mixed. They were worried about me being different – at school there were only two other vegetarians and I had to sit on a separate table from my classmates at lunch. It was a 'special vegetarian table'. Over the years I sat with kids of all ages, mainly older, and it was pretty bad in terms of social interaction. It can be so hard standing out, but I knew I was doing the right thing and soon the numbers on that table started to grow. Nothing to do with me, of course.

I think my parents were also slightly apprehensive about how they would feed me, as we pretty much ate meat with every meal back then. Would I be getting the correct nutrition? But they also understood where I was coming from, and maybe even thought it was cute that I loved animals so much I didn't want to eat them. They tried to get me to eat meat for a while, by putting it on my plate, but I just didn't, and they realised I wasn't going to go back on my decision.

So this moment was a real awakening in terms of meat and where it comes from, and realising I did not want to be part of this system of death. At this point I was still eating fish, eggs and dairy, as well as wearing animal products. I'd barely scratched the surface.

The next step I took was to go cruelty free with my make-up products in my early teens. I think the media caused this decision. In my lifetime, the two issues that have had huge campaigning focus are animal testing and the fur industry. I would say they've received the most media coverage thus far and are also the most frowned upon generally (along with poaching, fox hunting etc.). Animal testing for cosmetics had been banned in the EU in 2013, and that felt like a huge step forward (unfortunately, this is more complex than it seems and many well-known brands still test on animals worldwide. I explain this in more detail in the beauty section). The point is, I was aware of these two causes – and so much comes back to being conscious of the reality – and so I didn't want to participate in buying products that caused so much animal suffering.

The next awakening came in relation to fish. Why didn't I make the connection that fish are animals too, after giving up meat? It sounds weird, but I didn't really grasp that they were conscious beings. I almost thought of them like plants. I think that the more interaction I had with an animal, the more I saw it as alive – like the lambs – and fish just felt more distant. I appreciate that being close to animals growing up was and is a matter of chance and likely explains why many people lack that connection. How can you care about someone or something if you've never met or interacted with them?

There are also so many myths about fish that encourage us to view them differently, like the one about them having only a three-second memory, or that they don't feel pain. Neither of these is true.[3]

I think also that perhaps I just didn't want to look into it, as I did enjoy eating fish. I loved the taste and there was a part of me that worried about my health if I were to remove that food group from my diet completely. Maybe I knew, subconsciously, that it wasn't really OK, but didn't want to confront the ugly reality. Fish seem more removed from humanity than other animals; so felt much harder to connect to on a human level.

Awakenings

"

The next awakening came
in relation to fish – why didn't
I make the connection that
fish are animals too?

"

I had a lot of people calling me out on eating fish, asking, 'If you don't eat meat, why do you eat fish?' And this chipped away at me, to be honest. You sometimes try to defend yourself, and that starts this uneasy feeling that yes, something isn't quite right, and maybe there are things you should look into. But it's easier to ignore the feeling – especially when mainstream society is telling you that eating animals is the normal thing to do and that you need animal products to be strong and healthy. I already felt so different to my friends; was I really ready to take that up a notch?

I remember so clearly my moment of awakening in relation to fish. I was filming for *Made in Chelsea* in New York, and we went into a crab shack to eat there. The tank at the front of the restaurant was piled with crabs and lobsters, crammed in together, barely any room to move. They looked terrified. I know that might sound crazy, but really – they looked so afraid. It was an extremely confronting moment: they were just there, waiting to be killed and it was happening right in front of me.

The chef came out to greet us, and so I asked him, 'They don't feel pain, do they?'

And he smiled (laughed actually) and said, 'Yes, they do and when you put them in the boiling water they scream!'

I felt sick. I think he must have seen the colour drain from my face. In that moment, all I wanted to do was take the tank and pour it into the sea, releasing those poor creatures. I left the restaurant with a loss of appetite and knew I would never eat lobster or crab again. How could

I never have thought about this before? How had it taken me *this* long to wake up?

Then I began to question things. If I felt this way about crabs and lobsters, what about fish? That led me to do some research of my own. I knew there were questions I needed to ask. I went on the PETA website and searched something like, 'Is eating fish cruel?'. A video came up. I told myself, OK, watch this video and be honest with your response. If you can honestly say, what I am doing in eating fish isn't wrong, then carry on. But if you feel bad you need to make a change.

So, I watched it. It was a short film about how animals – including humans – respond when they are afraid. There was a fish on the table, about to have its head chopped off. Its mouth opened and lettering came up on the screen, saying something like, 'Not all screams can be heard.' It sent shivers down my spine. I just knew I couldn't carry on eating fish. I do think if animals could talk to us, no animal would be killed. We use their silence against them.

Fish was off the menu, but I was still eating eggs and dairy. They were just the products of an animal, and didn't involve killing them – plus it was natural for chickens to lay eggs and cows to make milk, right? At this point, I still thought that vegans were pretty crazy, and that they had a narrow-minded view of farming. I'd grown up on a farm, and I didn't see overt cruelty there. I felt like vegans didn't know the reality of farming, and to be frank, that I knew better than them as I'd experienced it first-hand.

Then I went to a vegetarian restaurant called Mildreds with a childhood friend of mine. She'd been one of the

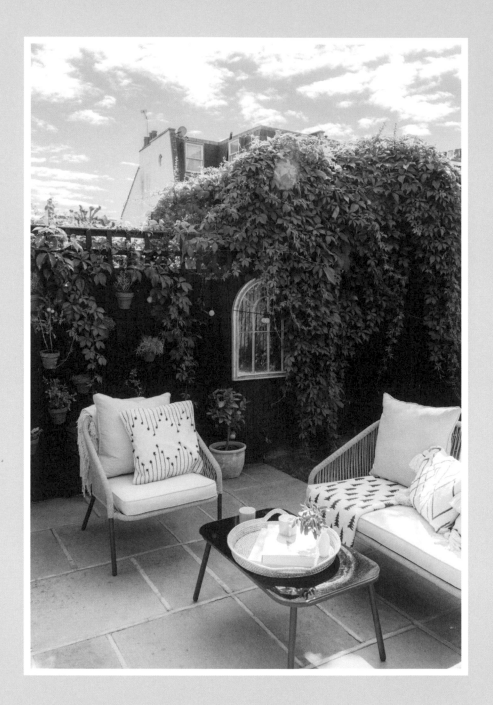

biggest meat eaters when we were growing up; she had never even considered going veggie. Over dinner, she told me she was now vegan. I was gobsmacked. I felt she was one of the last people in the world who would ever say those words to me!

She explained she had watched a documentary called *Cowspiracy*, and had decided to go vegan for environmental reasons. She insisted that I watch it, telling me it would convince me to go vegan as well.

I watched it, but I was still unsure what the problem was with eating dairy and eggs.

Then that night, I had a dream. I dreamt that I was a cow (I have very vivid dreams, I'm one of those) and I went through a pregnancy and gave birth to my baby calf. I was so in love with my baby. Then it got snatched away from me, to be killed, and I was trapped being a milking machine. I know it might sound a bit bonkers, but I really do see this dream as some sort of spiritual awakening.

I woke up, terrified and desperately upset, turned to my partner and told him all about it. He comforted me, telling me that this was just a dream and that this kind of thing doesn't happen in real life, so I shouldn't worry about it. But I couldn't shake off how vivid the dream had been and how much it made sense. I googled it, and pages and pages of results came up, confirming that a cow must be pregnant to produce milk, that in most farming systems female cows are artificially inseminated every year, that they are pregnant for nine months (just like humans), that their calves are taken away from them less than twenty-four hours after they are born, and many more horrors.

I cut out dairy the next day. I *loved* dairy. But I could no longer condone my obsession with these kinds of foods: they weren't worth more than the life of another being.

Eggs were next. Now, even at this point, I was convinced eggs were fine. I'd tweeted about giving up dairy and then loads of vegans were like, What about eggs? I sighed and probably rolled my eyes, convinced they didn't know the truth of it. It was natural for chickens to lay eggs – we'd had them on the farm, and I knew that they laid eggs naturally! It wasn't forced. It was just what they did.

I could no longer condone my obsession with these kinds of foods.

Then I googled it because so far the vegans had been right. I thought well, these vegans aren't all that stupid so maybe I should actually investigate this one too – and the vegans were right all along. Egg farming is inherently cruel as an industry. It doesn't matter if you buy free range or factory farmed; male chicks, who are of no use for egg or meat production, are killed almost immediately after hatching. They are either thrown into an industrial grinder or gassed to death. Around *seven billion* a year. It is shocking and definitely not common knowledge.

I probably had a few slip-ups in terms of what I ate after this point, especially when I was out and in contact with mac and cheese. But I felt so guilty I stopped. It didn't feel good to eat these things any more; they were tainted and quite honestly, the richness had started to make me feel a bit sick.

I came to question my clothing and fashion accessories about six months after eggs – I just don't think I was ready to before, as I'd changed so much in my life already. But then along came more things that opened my eyes.

I'd bought a pair of Chanel boots that I absolutely loved. Everyone was telling me how great they looked. Then I looked at the label and it said 'calf leather'. I was horrified. But, I'll be honest, at that point I just didn't want to think about it. Yes, I was still being selfish and ignoring what my gut instinct was telling me, because I was also relatively materialistic at that time in my life. Designer items were everything to me. I continued wearing the boots.

But another massive wake-up call awaited me. I'd entered into a deal with a luxury car brand – I had the most gorgeous car as part of it, with leather interiors. It was a car I could have only ever dreamed of owning. People were calling me out on it, saying it was made of dead cows, but I still convinced myself it was kind of OK, and blocked out that all-important gut feeling. I presumed they were just jealous haters and stayed firm with the mind frame that leather was a by-product of the meat industry. I was already fighting the cause by not eating meat.

I visited the factory to see how the cars were made, and the workers were showing me all the aspects of how a luxury car is crafted. I remember they showed me the leather that's used for the interiors, and just handling it felt a bit weird.

Looking for some reassurance, I asked the designer, 'Where does the leather come from? It's a by-product of the meat industry, right?'

He shook his head. 'No. The leather has to be absolutely pristine, we can't risk any nicks to the skin so it comes from specific farms.' He paused, before telling me, 'About eight cows died for that car.'

In a state of shock, I got into the car and drove home. I was suddenly overwhelmingly aware of the smell of the leather seats, of those eight cows that had died. I realised I was being materialistic and selfish, and so I walked away from working with that brand and gave back the car. I bought another one with a leather-free interior. Although it wasn't nearly as luxurious as the previous car I had been driving, I felt slightly better about it. My conscience was a little more at ease and that is a nice feeling.

I suppose from then on, it just became a question of, 'Can I wear this with confidence that it's morally right?' I kept getting called out on things on social media, and that did make me think about my responsibility as someone with a public profile to do the right thing, and not promote items that I knew were cruel. So the boots were given away, and I got rid of nearly all of my expensive designer handbags as well – I still cared a lot about that stuff back then. It was hard letting go, but each time I did it, I knew I'd done the right thing and felt a little lighter in general.

For me, it's about peeling back the layers of social conditioning and going back to my original instinct of being that child who didn't want to eat meat. Who couldn't hurt another living being intentionally.

How
to Get
Started

'm often asked for tips on how to get started on being vegan. It will be different for everyone but I hope the following principles are helpful:

- Start questioning your beliefs and undoing your conditioning.

- Find your 'why'.

- Educate yourself.

Beliefs

As soon as I started questioning why we treated animals in this way, I couldn't stop. I began to think a lot about where those beliefs came from – who or what programmed us to think like this? If we can understand this, we can start to challenge our beliefs and create new ones.

Upbringing

As you will have seen from my own story, the way that you have been raised can have a huge impact on your core being. Your parents will teach you the difference between 'right' and 'wrong' as well as set an example of how you should behave in many life situations. Confusingly, some of the lessons I was taught growing up were, 'you should not harm others', 'violence is wrong', 'compassion is good' and 'Pets are like family'. Even though eating any animal product will conflict with all of the above in one way or another.

It's about universal love and respect for all living beings.

Animals are more complex souls than many seem to believe. We are *all* animals, but we have been conditioned into treating some species as 'lesser' than others. Studies have proven that farm animals, such as pigs, are some of the most intelligent species on the planet, for example[4]. But I now think the whole way in which we learn to put animals in a hierarchy is wrong. It's so illogical to love and do anything for your pet dog, and yet consume meat products from another sentient being. Ultimately, what makes sense is to treat all animals equally. It's not about comparing whether a fish feels more than a chicken, or if a pig is more intelligent than a dog – it's about universal respect and love for all living beings.

Whilst there may be a conflict in how you are raised in terms of your morals and how you are taught to act and what you are told to eat, I wouldn't see this as a reflection of your parents. Unfortunately they are just another cog in the system. Their parents would have raised them in the same manner, and it takes something big to make you snap out of how you have been conditioned to be. After all, parents learn how to be parents from *their* parents and the people around them when they grew up. They probably think they have been doing the right thing, and might find it challenging when you come to your own conclusions about what is morally correct.

It can be difficult when your beliefs are challenged or aren't in line with those of the people close to you, or if they are challenged. My mum and sister are now vegan as well, which is great, but I do understand how hard and isolating it can be to be 'the different one'. Make sure to surround yourself with people and influences that support your journey.

Marketing

A huge amount of money has gone into perpetuating myths about animal products, so that we have certain associations with them that are hard to shake. Notions such as 'strong men eat meat' and 'milk is good for your bones' were and still are successful ways of encouraging people to buy these products, even though these myths have been dispelled in recent years. (For example, the Olympic gold medallist Carl Lewis says he got his best sporting results after turning vegan[5]).

If you walk down the street, or turn on the TV or even the radio, it's pretty hard to avoid some sort of sales campaign for animal products. Think of burger adverts – the glistening burger tucked inside a bun, with a catchy soundtrack, or chicken adverts, the nuggets sizzling in oil as they are fried. Serious money is spent on creating this image, and creating this desire for meat in consumers.

Then we have the images created about the means of production, which again will have been strategised by whole marketing teams. Whether it's a burger business telling you how well they take care of the animals used on their menus or milk companies telling you how their cows are 'happy' cows that live in grassy fields, we are constantly being fed lies. And this has been drilled into us, for decades . . . No wonder we've got to this point.

One advert that sticks out in my mind from my childhood is the Dairylea Dunkers commercial. A lot of their marketing involved cartoon cows looking happy and finding ways to get the products into children's hands. I for one definitely fell for this marketing. I felt like it was

what the cows wanted; they wanted me to eat these products! When of course, the likelihood is very much the opposite.

Another one that stands out to me is the laughing cow, a brand that creates dairy products. When writing this book I went back and reminded myself what these adverts used to look like. Picture this: cows dancing around with heaps of cheese, mixing it up and serving it whilst laughing and even singing. Talk about false advertising . . .

We forget the reality of where these products comes from.

I'll paint you a picture. A cow is forcibly impregnated with bull sperm using a device or the hand and arm of a human. Unpleasant, and you wouldn't wish it on anyone, especially without consent: there's a word we use for an act like that when it is happening to humans. But it doesn't stop there. The cow then has to go nine months growing a baby, only for it to be taken away the day or day after it is born so that the mother can be used to pump milk that can then be sold to humans. This has to happen four or five times before the cow is deemed 'spent'. Male calves who can't be used for milk are either killed shortly after birth or sent away for veal.

Doesn't sound very similar to the advert I described.

For me, advertising and marketing like this is an extremely dangerous tool, especially when used on children. It will not only encourage people and children to buy and eat these products, but it totally confuses kids as to where their food comes from. It tricks them into thinking there is no conflict between loving animals and eating them, as it gives the impression that the animals are happy and treated well.

Then there's clothing. We are so conditioned to wearing leather, thinking it is the 'best' choice for shoes and jackets, that we forget the reality of where these products comes from. Brands want you to do this. It's best for them if you just see the nice end product, beautifully displayed and on sale in a shop. They don't want you to think about what exactly has happened to get that product to you, because if you knew the truth, you'd almost certainly be put off. We are also sold the idea that silk and wool are luxurious, that these are 'natural' choices that offer us the best performance. But why do we think like this? When the production of these products causes the suffering and exploitation of animals.

My message to you is: don't trust the marketing. Look behind the label. There is usually a reason why means of production are hidden – that's because companies know most people would be put off if they were aware of what goes on.

"

Just because something has a history does not mean we should continue it, exactly as it has always been done.

"

Tradition

Every culture has its own traditions and sadly some of these involve some form of animal cruelty. These traditions occur all over the world, with some countries differing in which animals they use. We often carry on traditions simply because it's what has always been done, without questioning why. To question it would be deemed disrespectful.

For example, we eat animals on special occasions such as Christmas, but *why?* Meat might have been included as historically it was too expensive to be a daily food and thus formed part of a celebration, but there is actually no ongoing reason to do this. But once an emotional attachment is formed to a ritual, it's very hard to break: we don't want to lose the happiness, excitement: sense of reward, that have become attached to that tradition, and we often take comfort in the sense of history a tradition has. But I assure you, it's perfectly possible to enjoy these same emotions and celebrations without an animal suffering for it.

The same goes for various sports and pastimes that are seen as traditional: hunting, bull fighting, horse racing, to name just a few. People defend these because they are 'what has always happened'; they are part of a nation's cultural identity; spectators enjoy the excitement and thrill that they feel when watching these sports.

Just because something has a history does not mean we should continue it, exactly as it has always been done. Society has always evolved and changed, and we should include our traditions in this, seeing them for what they really are.

There is so much illogical thinking when you start to consider traditions. For example, a lot of people are horrified by the idea of dog fighting or badger baiting, but watch the Grand National, in which horses are whipped and kicked around a dangerous course, often resulting in injury and even death.

So, start questioning the reasons why a tradition is upheld. 'Because that's just how it is,' isn't a good enough answer. You can absolutely find new ways to bring people together in a shared experience, without causing animal suffering.

Something I hear over and over again is the idea that it's natural for us to eat and use animals – and if you google this kind of thing you get pages and pages of conflicting arguments about what humans 'naturally' eat. I would counter that and suggest there is nothing natural about intensive farming, or forcing a cow to be pregnant almost constantly.

So much of what we do *isn't* 'natural' – so why continue to justify choices in this way, when it causes so much harm and suffering?

Find your 'why'

Once you begin unpicking the way in which your beliefs have been programmed, it's good to get your positive motivation sorted. Think of it every time you make a vegan choice. Sometimes it'll be as simple as reaching for another product in the supermarket; other times you might have to make more of an effort, or do more research, but if you understand your personal motivation behind these decisions, you will find the strength to make the right choice.

There are three main motivations for becoming vegan.

Ethics

This was the overwhelming reason why I became vegan. Simply, it was for the animals. The more I thought about it, and began examining my beliefs and discovering more about the reality of what consuming animals really entails, I just couldn't do it. I love animals – why would I eat them? And even if I didn't feel such a strong connection to animals, I believe that animals have a right to life, and to freedom, just like us. They're here with us, not for us.

There is a huge amount of evidence to suggest that animals suffer horribly when they are bred, born, raised and killed for human consumption. To me, this just is not right – to cause these living beings great suffering when we simply don't need to. Imagine you were brought into existence purely to be killed or used, would you be happy about this? Sometimes animals are killed the same day they are born.

I also strongly believe that animals shouldn't be used as commodities. It feels very wrong to be making money out of them, by whatever means: using them for food, clothing, or other uses. They don't get a choice in the matter and if they could speak I don't think it would take a huge amount of imagination to figure out what they would prefer. Let's not use the fact that they cannot speak

against them. We go on about how intelligent we are as a species so let's use our intelligence to work out what they would want rather than using it to find ways to hurt them and make money out of them, especially if we are lucky enough to have a choice as to how we make money.

"

The idea of a diet that avoids the consumption of animal products is ancient.

"

Although the term 'veganism' was coined in 1944, the idea of a diet that avoids the consumption of animal products is ancient – and do tell this to anyone who thinks veganism is a modern 'fad' that will pass. One of the first mentions of vegetarianism in Europe was by the Greek philosopher Pythagoras, around 500 BC. He promoted kindness amongst all species. Followers of Buddhism, Hinduism and Jainism have also followed a vegetarian diet since ancient times, in the belief that we should not inflict suffering onto other beings.

"The greatness of a nation and its moral progress can be judged by the way its animals are treated. I hold that the more helpless a creature the more entitled it is to protection by man from the cruelty of humankind."
Gandhi

"Compassion for animals is intimately associated with goodness of character, and it may be confidently asserted that he who is cruel to animals cannot be a good man."
Arthur Schopenhauer, 18th Century philosopher

"I have since an early age abjured the use of meat, and the time will come when men will look upon the murder of animals as they look upon the murder of man."
Leonardo Da Vinci

Although the main ethical reason for veganism is to do with animals, humans also suffer in the supply chain. Slaughterhouse work is considered the most dangerous occupation in America and is often carried out by the most vulnerable groups in society. Injury, including serious injury resulting in amputation, is common. Then there is the mental toll of working in a death machine. Studies have shown how workers become traumatised by constantly killing animals.[6]

So why would we ask other human beings, as well as animals, to suffer just so we can eat animal products?

I also think about the ethics of what kind of planet we are leaving for the next generation.

When I consider the prospect of having children, I think about the world they will grow up in. Will it be a world

where we still treat other beings on the planet with no mercy? Where we kill fifty-six billion animals a year to shove in our faces even though we have alternative options of food for survival and pleasure? Where we devastate natural habitats, killing many other animals along the way, just so we can breed more animals we like the taste of?

I don't want my children, or anyone's, to grow up in a world like this. I want them to be able to swim in oceans that are thriving with life, and to enjoy the beauty and colour, just like I did when I was growing up. I want them to walk in beautiful countryside that teems with all kinds of living beings. I want them to be compassionate and to witness compassion wherever they go. I don't want them to live in an evil, grey, dying world.

Health

This wasn't my main reason for going vegan, but I see it as an added benefit, for sure. My opinion is that it's too simplistic to say a vegan diet is or isn't healthy: there are so many factors involved. I will say, it's not an automatic benefit. You need to do it right. If you go for a plant-based, wholefood diet, that's one of the healthiest diets you can have[7]. When I first went vegan, there was very little vegan junk food, so I naturally ate very healthily. I lost so much weight off my face and body, and had so much energy – I was like a different human.

If you look at heart disease, diabetes and cancer, these all have a risk factor linked to a diet high in animal products, and there is a lot of evidence to show the benefits of eating a variety of fruit and vegetables, in terms of vitamins, minerals and fibre.[8]

There are some good documentaries you can watch, which explain more about this, such as *What the Health* and *Forks over Knives.*

Interestingly, one study showed an increase in exercise performance on a vegan diet compared to an omnivorous one.[9] Vegan athletes like Venus Williams, Lewis Hamilton and Novak Djokovic just go to show how strong and healthy you can be on a vegan diet.

"

I want children to walk in beautiful countryside that teems with ... living beings.

"

I would also say, think of the health benefits in terms of what you are *not* consuming. So many animal products come laced with hormones and antibiotics. Antibiotic use in animals is a huge factor in growing antibiotic resistance around the globe, which poses one of the greatest threats to our health.

Animals on farms often suffer from many health problems; even on organic farms, the animals are often sick. If they have tumours, these will often be cut out of the meat before it's consumed. I dare you to do a Google image search. Chickens in the US are washed in chlorine, and huge amounts of artificial growth hormones are used in American cattle. The reason for this all comes down to profit – it boosts the amount of meat that a farmer can sell per animal.

I know we still use chemicals on plant foods – I'd advise anyone to buy organic as much as possible, but even if that's not possible, you can still remove a lot of pesticide residue by washing the surface of your produce. Washing meat is not going to remove the substances that have been flowing through that animal's veins and flesh.

At the time of writing this, we are in the middle of a global pandemic. Although the origins of Covid-19 are not yet known, it is believed to have originated from a wet market in China. Before this, many other health scares (such as BSE/mad cow disease, bird flu, SARS and swine flu) have had their origins in farming practices, and likely spread through animal markets and livestock rearing. The way in which animals are kept cramped together is a perfect environment for a virus to spread.[10]

I am no expert, but we need to look urgently at how our abuse of animals within agriculture is creating enormous health hazards for humans and how our eating habits are quite literally affecting *everyone* in a negative way.

Environment

Whilst the beginning of my own veganism was more about thinking of animals, the whole concept of the environment has become a bigger and bigger factor in how I approach the world. It is simply something that we all need to care about as it affects all of us, regardless of our values. We all have to think about it and take action. When I think about bringing children into this world I wonder – how can people justify destroying the planet for the next generation, when they can't be bothered to make changes?

I know that environmental concerns are a huge reason for many people in going vegan. Cattle farming is a major factor in rising emissions. As well as CO_2, it releases methane and nitrous oxide – which is a lot more deadly than CO_2.[11]

Industrial-scale cattle farming also has an enormous effect on species extinction, as humans destroy forests and natural habitats to make room for cattle grazing.[12]

The use of land for cattle in the Brazilian Amazon is the largest driver of deforestation in the world. Between 1988 and 2014, 480,000km of deforested territory in the Amazon has become pasture for cattle. That's equivalent to five times the size of Portugal. [13]

Other forms of environmental pollution from farming are also causing enormous problems. For example, slurry can leak into waterways, causing great damage to river ecosystems.[14] In terms of fishing, the image of just taking a few fish from the ocean isn't true. The whole infrastructure of fishing is incredibly damaging to marine

"

Environmental concerns are a huge reason for many people in going vegan.

"

habitats, as well as devastating to fish populations. A Greenpeace study found that lost and abandoned fishing gear makes up the majority of large plastic pollution in the oceans. More than 640,000 tonnes of nets, lines, pots and traps used in commercial fishing are dumped and discarded in the sea every year, the same weight as 55,000 double-decker buses.[15]

This 'ghost gear' has another devastating effect, as so many fish and other sea creatures become tangled in it. In 2018, according to the same Greenpeace study, about three hundred sea turtles were found dead as a result of entanglement in ghost gear off the coast of Oaxaca, Mexico. We are emptying our seas: a recent analysis of the Mediterranean showed that 93 per cent of the assessed fish stocks are over-exploited[16]. That's before we consider the devastating effect of 'bycatch' – the 'non-target' creatures that are caught up in fishing. The statistics are unbelievable: about 40 per cent of fish catch worldwide is unintentionally caught. Those animals are thrown back into the sea, either dead or dying. Killed accidentally each year are:

- 300,000 small whales and dolphins

- 250,000 endangered loggerhead turtles and critically endangered leatherback turtles

- 300,000 seabirds, including seventeen albatross species[17]

I'll be honest: there are also big questions to answer regarding the production of certain vegan foods. Avocados, which are so popular at the moment, are linked to deforestation and huge water consumption in Mexico. Almonds are similarly water-thirsty and are linked to damaging environments in California where the majority are grown. However, the science shows that the environmental impact of almond milk, for example, is still less than that of dairy milk.[18]

Often people will throw out these accusations when they hear you are vegan, so be prepared! This is where the principle of conscious effort comes in for me. It's about constantly educating yourself in terms of what you consume, and working out where you can do better and cause less harm to the environment.

Motivation

Once you've made the decision, for whatever reasons, to go vegan, how do you *stay* vegan? Everyone is different. I am quite a determined, stubborn person (you may have noticed) and when I decide on something, it's quite rare I change my mind. But I know other people are different!

What I'd say if you're tempted, or you take a step back, is just keep going and don't beat yourself up if you slip up here and there. I wanted to share my journey with you to show that it didn't happen overnight; it wasn't perfect.

Try these tips:

- Constantly remind yourself of why you are doing this. Make notes, or rewatch a documentary. My top three are *Cowspiracy*, *Forks Over Knives* and *Earthlings*. *Game Changers* is also really good, but there are so many great ones.

- Keep the 'why' in mind. Once you start blocking this out it's likely you'll lose motivation.

- Follow people on Instagram who will positively reinforce your decision. Check out: livekindly-co, vegancommunity, earthlinged, jamesaspey, plantbasednews.

- Get inspired – thinking about new recipes, for example, is a great way to stop thinking about what you can't have, and switch your focus to trying something new.

- Don't stop following upsetting pages. I know it can be horrendous and emotional – sometimes I cry for hours about what I'm seeing – but we can't close our eyes to the truth. Sometimes when I link or post something, people will reply saying, 'I don't want to see that!' Believe me, I don't want to see it either, but it exists and we have to face the reality.

- Don't let the haters get you down, if people are querying your choices or being unsupportive. Remember why you are doing this. Remember that it is your decision about how you live your life. Also, people sometimes criticise you when they are defensive about their own way of living – it's easier to attack someone else than look honestly at your own shortcomings.

- If you need to go slow, go slow – but get there. There is no downside. You're helping yourself, the animals and the environment.

Family, friends and dating

One of the hardest things about going vegan can actually be the reactions of the people closest to you. The ones that you love the most and whose approval you value above anyone's.

When I went vegan, which as we know was not a huge step for me having already been veggie for many years, I didn't expect the reaction I received. My family were worried for my health; they thought I would get sick more (I used to be ill a lot of the time). My sister, who was also veggie, said, 'I think it's a bit extreme'.

I knew that these concerns all came from a lack of understanding regarding veganism and I didn't let it upset or worry me. Personally, I have a thing with liking to prove

people wrong and when I decide to do something I rarely let anything or anyone stand in my way.

However, I get so many messages from people that don't deal with it in the same way, and get massively affected by the opinions of their friends and family. I get this – it can be disheartening, especially when you may be super excited about this new and positive journey. The support of those closest to you can only uplift and encourage you and when you don't get this it can be very disappointing and even upsetting. It can make you feel like you no longer belong . . . and although that may sound dramatic, I know there are thousands of children going through this all the time with their families and that breaks me. To want to live a kinder and more conscious life that will benefit animals, the planet and your health is not only a really great thing but it is also extremely brave in a world where the majority of people do not choose to live this way. To stand out from 'the masses' and become part of 'a minority' is never easy. But I promise you, it will be worth it and there are certain ways of overcoming uncomfortable situations.

Then there's dating, a subject I get asked about a lot. When I first started dating my boyfriend he was a fully blown carnivore (we're talking a freezer full of meat and eating large amounts of animal protein daily) and I was a vegetarian. When I went vegan it began to bother me more and more that he was still eating animals. Living together intensified this feeling, cooking with the same pans and sharing space in the kitchen. It began to really upset me – I was choosing to live one way and he was choosing to live the opposite. I predicted issues for our future, we had different values and would likely have different opinions on how to raise children. Luckily, he was open minded enough to watch some of the documentaries I had and felt inclined to start making some changes. He started by cutting out red meat (for health reasons) and slowly cut out chicken.

I know deep down that a huge part of these decisions was in support of me, but I also know now that this is a lifestyle he whole heartedly agrees with. He's mostly plant based, eating animal products such as dairy or fish on very rare occasions. This works for us and who knows – he may increase his level of veganism in the future. What will work for you may be completely different, but I will say I think it is important to be with someone who has the same values as you, regardless of your diet. If you're wanting to raise your kids vegan, don't put this conversation off until *after* you have children. These conversations are important and can affect your lives.

The most important thing is that you support each other's choices. Plus – there are vegan dating apps now! So never lose hope that there is someone out there just as passionate about this as you, if that's what you're looking for.

Lead by example

The best thing you can do, is 'do you'. Live your best life! People will notice and they will likely want in on it. By showing how amazing veganism is and how great it makes you feel, you are literally the best advert for becoming vegan. If you serve up great food that just so happens to be vegan people will start to see it as a positive choice,

rather than focusing on what you *can't* have as part of a vegan diet.

Educate

I made my mum and sister watch the documentaries I had watched because I knew they loved animals just as much as I did. The only reason they weren't vegan was because they didn't truly understand what veganism was and how animals were suffering for every kind of animal product. I had friends that were huge meat eaters that also loved animals; some took days to convert, others years. But ultimately, if you are against animal cruelty then veganism is the best option for you. End of.

Being pushy doesn't always work. It worked with my mum and sister because that's just the relationship that we have and now they are vegan and would never look back. With others, it can push them the other way, and make them resistant to change.

These days, unless I'm posting on my social media channels, I like to be invited before I preach. It's not something I start doing because someone across the table from me is eating an animal. Nine out of ten times, it just annoys people. Remember, most people *hate* being told what to do and they also hate change.

A lot of the time I don't even bring veganism up unless someone asks – and it's usually questions that are trying to catch me out, like 'But why don't you drink milk, cows have to be milked?' or 'Eating free-range eggs doesn't hurt the chicken,' or maybe the classic 'But where do you

"

If you are against animal cruelty veganism is the best option for you.

"

get your protein from?'. So long as you have done your research (or read this book) then most questions won't faze you and you can politely and calmly reply with the correct information. No need to get sassy (although this may be harder for some) as again this will get people's backs up. We're not trying to piss people off, we're trying to recruit vegans here. If your blood is boiling, always think of the bigger picture.

CEREAL

In this volume, we look towards **Korea**. We explore the architecture of **Itami Jun**, the photography of **Koo Bohnchang** and the **Dansaekhwa** art movement. We converse with **David Chang** and **Eunju Park**, visit **Charlotte Perriand's Méribel** chalet, walk with **Aesop**, and share our cultural guide to Seoul.

VOL 18 S/S 2020 £12

Food

Most people think of veganism in relation to diet first, and if you're going vegan, it will probably be the place you start. As well as being essential for survival, food is central to every human culture. It brings us together as a community and culinary traditions are some of our most emotionally powerful and binding.

We involve food in so many 'traditional' scenarios that I think have helped us stay connected to where we started. I also think religious practices, rituals and celebrations play a huge part in the way that we eat. I know I used to love all the food on Christmas Day and Easter, and enjoyed the way that it tasted. We think of those sorts of events as 'holidays' where we spend time with our families and most of us have time off work. The thought of changing anything, such as swapping out real turkey for vegan turkey, can at first appear like it will change the whole experience. But really, any happy ceremony or traditional celebration should never have to be fun or enjoyable because of there being a dead animal on the table. Surely if we actually saw that process from start to finish, we would realise there is really *nothing* happy about it. Try swapping in a vegan alternative and you could find your family may not even notice the difference. The alternatives are great these days, it's truly amazing what can be created with plants.

A brief history

There is so much complicated and often conflicting research about the human diet. About if it's 'natural' for us to eat meat, about when we started doing so, and if it's necessary for our health.

The diet of the very earliest humans probably contained large quantities of fruit, leaves, flowers, bark and insects, as well as nuts and seeds and roots and tubers. Around 2.6 million years ago, some early humans began incorporating meat and marrow from a variety of animals into their diet, which we know from bones with butchery marks on them. But already, you can see how the concept of a 'natural' diet is a hard one to follow. It depends how far back you go. The fact is, humans are incredibly adaptable, and our diet reflects this – we survive on what's available. In terms of hunting down animals for food, as opposed to scavenging, the earliest evidence for this dates to about five hundred thousand years ago.[19]

"

Try swapping in a vegan alternative and you could find your family may not even notice the difference.

"

This was when we were dependent on our environment – and what was available – for survival. When people start talking about whether it's 'natural' or not for humans to eat meat, for me that isn't the point. The point is that we now have a huge amount of choice in what we need – regardless of what our ancestors consumed, there is simply no reason for us to mindlessly keep continuing to eat animal products, especially if we are able to survive without them.

I'll also add, the way in which our ancestors would have consumed meat is unrecognisable from the industrialised farming practices we see today. The idea that these practices are 'natural' is crazy. For example, wild chickens naturally lay ten to fifteen eggs per year, and can live for up to six years. A farmed chicken might produce three hundred eggs per year, but will usually be slaughtered after twelve to eighteen months.

Farming

The history of agriculture is different all around the world. It's thought that humans farmed grains before they farmed animals, starting in about 9500 BC.

Depending on world location, the first animals to be farmed included cattle, sheep and goats, as well as chickens and pigs in other regions. They were used in various ways – some animals, including horses and oxen, for labour; others for the products they produced (eggs and milk), before ultimately being killed for meat. Sheep were farmed not only for their flesh, but also for their wool and skins. Cattle were (and still are) used for their flesh, milk, skin and sometimes even labour, taking on the role of horses.

It is thought that these particular species were chosen because herds of animals were the easiest to control. These animals, including pigs, horses and chickens, were then domesticated and humans quickly began to control not only where they were kept, but also what they ate and even when they bred (not to mention, when their lives would end).

Depending on where in the world you look, horses have been used for manual labour, but also for their meat. Many meat-eaters recoil at the thought of eating horse meat, but to me this is so illogical. I actually get quite frustrated when people are disgusted by what animals are eaten in

other countries, without looking at and thinking about their own eating habits. In countries where that tradition has continued, such as France and Italy, there is no taboo around horse meat. It just goes to show how much our tastes are developed by the culture we grow up in. Incidentally, many countries that do not eat horse meat export horses to countries that do, chasing a profit. For example, horse meat generally isn't eaten in the States, but Texas exports a lot of horses for slaughter to Mexico. It's illogical and immoral.

Different techniques and new technologies have changed farming enormously. During the Industrial Revolution in the UK, selective breeding saw new types of sheep and cow emerge. Sheep were bred to produce large quantities of fine wool, and cows began to be bred exclusively for beef (as opposed to labour as well). Again, I'll make the point that this is hardly 'natural' – it's humans choosing what animals to breed together to fit a certain set of characteristics, regardless of what other problems this might cause.

When refrigeration became widely used in the early twentieth century, and transport was improved, farmers were able to refrigerate animal flesh and export it more widely. Meat became more affordable and readily available, and consequently consumer appetites increased. Meat production today is almost five times higher than it was sixty years ago.[20]

Farmers turned to this profitable way of making a living, and these businesses were passed down through generations. There is an enormous emotional pressure to continue what your parents have built, and it can be difficult for farmers to suddenly question the morals and ethics behind what they are doing – it's all they have ever known. It feels like it would be wrong for them to leave this way of life.

" I am hopeful that the tide is turning.

"

Now, we are also seeing big business get involved in farming. Enormous farms raise animals on an industrial scale, with profit as the priority. Welfare conditions are often horrendous, with animals crowded into enclosures with barely any light or space to move. Mutilation is rife – to prevent animals injuring each other (as they don't have space, and are incredibly stressed), their teeth and claws are clipped, often without pain relief, and tail docking is frequent, even when it's meant to be illegal.[21] These farms often receive vast subsidies to continue producing meat and animal products. You can see how broken the system is.

Just imagine if we had some of the same infrastructure and investment around vegan produce, and how much would change. There are hopeful signs, demand for beef and pork has levelled off in the US and Europe[22]. More and more people are swapping out meat products for vegetarian or vegan meals – in 2019, one in four food product launches in the UK were vegan[23].

I am hopeful that the tide is turning, and it's great you want to be a part of it.

So, where to start in changing your diet?

A practical guide to a vegan diet

I know many of you reading this will be well on the path to veganism, but if you're just starting to look for ways to make a change, or are struggling to switch fully, then this section is full of practical tips.

When changing from eating a 'standard' diet including animal products to eating a diet that is more in line with your beliefs it can be a bit of a shock to the system. For me, I had already been pescatarian most of my life and vegetarian for the last few years, so all that remained for me to line up with my morals was to stop eating dairy and eggs. It may seem like this is pretty straightforward, but for someone who ate these products for breakfast, lunch and dinner, I was slightly stuck on where to go. Back then, in 2016, there were very few products on the market to replace your daily staples. There was also little to no information online. Now we go to the supermarkets and can't avoid the abundance of vegan alternatives. You may already drink a plant-based milk and you may even eat vegan meals without meaning to, just because they taste good and are easy to find.

It is so heartening to see these changes seeping into mainstream society. We need to make sure veganism isn't just a trend, and is here to stay – and the place to start this is in your own life. How do you make vegan changes stick?

---

1) The simplest step towards changing up what you eat is to have a fridge clear-out – start afresh. Get rid of the animal products from your kitchen and replace them with your new vegan-friendly alternatives. It's easier to avoid temptation altogether than resist it when it's under your nose – if you don't have the choice to reach for dairy milk in the fridge, you won't!

   I understand not all finances may allow for this, so another option is to replace as you go – this will also limit food waste. When something runs out, say your butter for instance, instead of buying that same dairy butter again, choose a vegan alternative. You can apply this rule to pretty much anything except for eggs. Right now, as I write this book, there aren't easily accessible egg replacements in the UK that you can cook in the morning unless you scramble tofu or ackee. However, there are definitely alternatives that you can use for baking such as flaxseed, banana and vegetable oil.

2) Get inspired! Once you've got your head around eating a vegan diet you may want to start following some vegan food bloggers online so you can be inspired about what to cook. I still find this a really

useful tool as it opens up my eyes to how inventive we can really be with plant-based foods. After a few months or so, it will become your new normal and you'll probably start wondering what took you so long. Yes, you can still eat 'meaty meals', yes you can still cook for dinner parties, yes you can still get takeaways and yes, you can still enjoy date night.

Find recipes that are easy for you, and get your basics sorted. Staples for breakfast could be scrambled tofu on toast, avocado on toast, granola or overnight oats. For lunch, think about soups, pasta dishes and curries. For dinner you might try out a meat substitute with lots of well-seasoned veggies.

3) See it as a culinary adventure. One great thing I gained from eating solely plant foods for the last four years is that my palate has completely changed (for the better). I now have so much more appreciation for the natural flavours of fruit and vegetables. I know it sounds a bit ridiculous, but there are literally hundreds of thousands of different kinds of fruit and veg packed full of their own unique flavours – we are so lucky! I used to live off beige foods and cheese or eggs. I wasn't getting nearly enough nutrition and my palate was very basic.

Through cooking plant-based foods I have also learnt the importance of flavour and now I love cooking with herbs and spices. If you think about it, the reason people love the taste of meat and fish so much isn't because of the taste of the flesh itself, but because of how it has been seasoned or marinated. A lot of the time, you'll be able to replicate the dish you like with the same herbs and spices and sauces, just used on a vegan substitute.

4) If you start missing the foods you used to eat, remember that habits take time to break and you won't always feel like this. Think about what you're craving, and why. Is it the association of comfort? Is it what you always ate? A certain texture, like a creamy sauce? Once you've worked it out, then you can start finding a substitute. Vegan food can be whatever you want it to be.

5) Identify weak spots. Is it eating out? Being hungry on the way home from work? Hangovers? If you break your veganism, see it as learning. Why did you break it? What tempted you? Then use that evidence to do better next time, and plan for it. Get some vegan ready meals in the freezer so you're good to go as soon as you get in from work, or find a great vegan takeaway (most Indian or Thai places will have amazing vegan options). If you get tempted on the way home from work, make sure you have a vegan snack with you – I love vegan snack bars like Vive and Trek– or go for a healthy option like fruit or nuts. But make sure you plan!

Special events like Christmas, can be difficult to navigate and you may well be tempted into eating your old favourites. Again, planning is essential here. Work out your treats – the foods you can still have that give you that buzz of dopamine.[24]

Understanding cravings

I always say the first two weeks of being vegan are the hardest, just like with any addiction – and these kinds of foods can be addictive. Some studies have shown that dairy products such as cheese are somewhat addictive due to containing high levels of casein, the dominant protein in dairy.[25]

Dairy proteins inside cheese can act as mild opiates, creating cravings. Your body's reward system also releases dopamine when you satisfy these cravings, making a cycle. So when you think you can't live without cheese, it's because your brain is *telling* you you can't! But trust me, you can. And after a few months you may even forget why you ever liked cheese in the first place. I know I did. The thought of it now makes me feel a bit ill, especially when I found out that so many cows suffer from mastitis – a horrible infection and inflammation of their udders.

And the truth is that cheese alternatives these days are so good! Some may not taste exactly like the cheese you used to love (or were addicted to) but they definitely fill a cheese-shaped hole in your stomach, and they often have less fat and cholesterol. It's worth shopping around as much as you can, to find the brand that you most prefer – everyone's tastes are different.

Brands to try:

- Bella Cheeze
- Kinda Co.
- Follow Your Heart
- Sheese
- Cicioni
- Daiya
- Koko
- Morrisons own brand
- Mozzarisella
- New Roots
- Nutcrafter Creamery
- Violife
- Sainsbury's own brand
- Tesco own brand
- Tyne Chease
- VBites

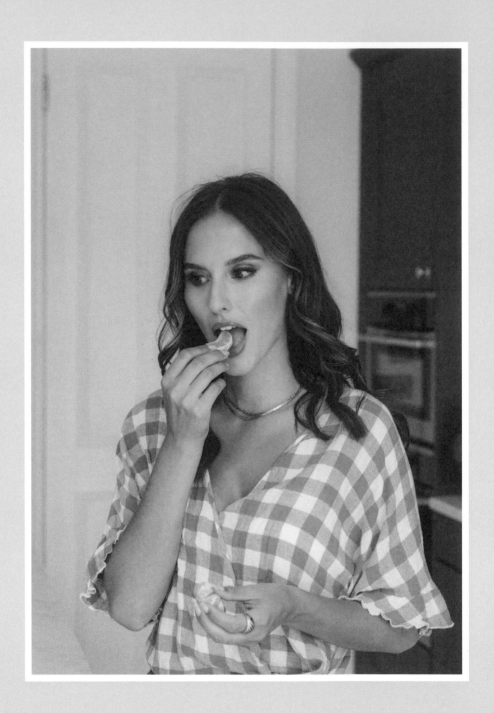

. . . see, told you you'd be spoiled for choice!

You can also try making your own vegan cheese – check out The Big Vegan Cheese Making Kit, or you can find loads of different recipes online.

Another great tip if you're craving cheese is nutritional yeast: sprinkle on pasta or add to recipes for that savoury spike of flavour. Nutritional yeast is high in nutritional properties: it contains B vitamins and trace elements, and is also a complete protein, meaning it contains all nine essential amino acids that humans require. One tablespoon contains two grams of protein, so it's an easy way to add high-quality protein to your plate.

Milk

This is another one that can be hard for people to give up, as we are so conditioned to having it as a food staple – drinking it in tea, coffee, on cereal and by itself. I'm happy to say there is again an abundance of options here: soya, rice, almond, oat, cashew, hemp, coconut and more.

There are also loads of brands producing these drinks now, including Alpro, Oatly, Plenish and Califa. A lot of supermarket own brands are doing vegan milks too.

A cost-effective option can be to make your own oat or nut milks. Again, there are guides to this online, and in my cookbook, *Feed Me Vegan*.

Your best bet is to try out the various milks and see what taste you prefer. I personally like soya milk in coffee and

tea, but others prefer oat (try the barista versions for a creamy texture). It all depends on what you want, really – oat milk has a slightly sweet taste, whereas soya milk can be blander. Almond milk is a bit more sour but is a favourite for the health conscious (not for the eco conscious). Nut milks tend to be very creamy. Do check if the milk has been sweetened or not; some people love this, others don't.

When it comes to baking, I tend to use soya milk but it also depends on what the recipe calls for, as each milk has individual properties.

"

Look at alternative breakfast options such as avocado toast, peanut butter with banana toast, smoothies, porridge and even vegan pancakes.

"

Eggs

In terms of cooking 'scrambled eggs' you may want to look at alternative breakfast options such as avocado toast, peanut butter with banana toast, smoothies, porridge and even vegan pancakes. Another option is to marinate some tofu to scramble and fry. There are many recipes for this online as well as in my recipe books *Feed Me Vegan* and *Feed Me Vegan For All Occasions*. Tofu scramble doesn't taste exactly like eggs, but it has a similar texture and is a yummy protein-packed breakfast to add to your plate in the morning.

Can I eat eggs from chickens I keep, or organic eggs?

Not if you're vegan. It's still taking something from an animal, and using animals for what they produce. There was a time when I believed I could continue eating a cruelty-free diet whilst still eating eggs. I had chickens on my farm and although they didn't live the most joyful of lives (cooped up in a pen with lots of other chickens they would regularly fight with) they didn't seem like they were enduring any cruelty whilst producing eggs. I had to research this further and that is when I discovered the horrible secrets behind the egg industry. This industry is a sexist one, towards male chicks. As they cannot produce eggs they are deemed useless and millions of chicks are either ground up alive, gassed to death or drowned every year. This an unavoidable cost of eating eggs, whether you buy free range/organic or not.

Even if you keep your own hens, what about when you're away from home? Personally, I think it's easier to avoid eggs altogether, especially when scientists can't agree on whether eggs are good for us or not[26] and the fact they are a chicken period (ew).

"

Try to buy organic and locally sourced.

"

Bigger picture

Although I went vegan for the animals I have learnt so much more about my impact on the planet throughout this journey. When buying fruit and veg I try to buy organic and locally sourced to help support my local farmers and to reduce my CO_2 emissions. Buying in season is a great way to keep your costs down and also to reduce the emissions caused by fruit and veg that have been transported over from other countries. I no longer buy fruit and veg from supermarkets, there's too much plastic and it's all totally unnecessary. You could try a local vegetable box too, which often come with recipe suggestions to try.

I try to grow herbs such as rosemary, oregano and thyme in my garden and my dream is to have my own vegetable patch one day! These are just some small changes you can make (while you're in the mood for change) to help reduce your impact.

Answering those awkward questions:
Isn't vegan food really expensive?

No, not necessarily! Some staples of a vegan diet are amongst the most affordable (think lentils, tins of beans, oats, potatoes, dried pasta etc.). Buying these staples in bulk will also help reduce costs, as will heading for supermarket own-brands (often just as tasty as branded products). You can also buy frozen veg instead of fresh, which keeps for longer.

There is generally a variety of pricing available with vegan products, so you can find something to suit every purse.

Buying staples in bulk will help reduce costs.

Shopping list ideas:

- Vegan butter

- Vegan milk

- Vegan cheese

- Nutritional yeast (amazing for adding savoury 'cheesy' flavour when cooking)

- Fruit & veg – cost depends on where you buy from, frozen can be cheaper

- Work out your favourite staples – mine are potatoes, broccoli, peppers, pak choi, carrots, spinach, kale, bananas, and frozen berries (amazing for smoothies)

- Carbs: rice, pasta, quinoa, lentils, beans, chickpeas

- Bread

- Oats

- Spices and herbs – this is a big one, so you can add loads of flavours. I'd suggest: cumin, oregano, ground coriander, cinnamon, ground ginger, basil, turmeric, chilli/cayenne, paprika, sage, thyme, rosemary, bay leaves. You can build up your supply gradually, of course

- Vegan stock

- Cans of coconut milk, chopped tomatoes – particularly handy for curries

- Tofu

- Vegan mince

- Vegan nuggets

- Vegan sausages

- Vegan burgers

Where do you get your protein from?

For some reason, people are obsessed with asking this question of vegans. Protein is quite misunderstood, and people often have the misconception that you can only get it from animal products. That isn't true. Protein is originally found in plants. Not all non-animal proteins are 'complete' proteins, meaning they don't contain sufficient amounts of all nine essential amino acids, whereas animal products can contain all nine in one. But, by eating a varied diet, you absolutely can get all nine amino acids you need.

Good protein sources for vegans include (but are not limited to):

- Quinoa

- Seitan

- Tofu

- Pulses, including lentils, chickpeas, garden peas, beans (all kinds, like black, pinto, kidney beans, etc.)

- Nuts and seeds – I am a huge fan of sprinkling seeds onto breakfast or into a smoothie. You can also include nut butters for a protein hit

- Oats – so versatile, and they provide 10g of protein per 100g serving

---

If you eat a balanced diet, you should be fine for your protein allowance – it really is in everything (including fruit and vegetables). You will only need to think consciously about protein if you're building muscle – so if you are working out loads and want to gain muscle, you probably will need a vegan protein powder. There are so many different delicious favours on the market; I love chocolate or salted caramel.

What about vitamins and minerals – how do you get everything you need?

A lot of people ask questions about what vitamins and minerals vegans are likely to be deficient in. Here's the way I see it. Someone could well be deficient in key vitamins and minerals if they're eating another diet. If someone is eating a lot of junk food that contains meat, they're very likely to be deficient in some nutrients.

It's something that should be thought about in general, not just in relation to vegan diets. Just because you're vegan doesn't mean you have to be absolutely perfect in consuming the exact right vitamins and minerals – you can't be a perfect human.

For me personally, eating a balanced, healthy diet is the best option. I make sure I have a balanced plate, with fibre, protein and carbohydrates. (I'm not afraid of carbs - they give you energy.)

The only thing that is substantially harder to get as a vegan is vitamin B12 – that is something to consciously add to your diet. It's an essential vitamin, that helps with making red blood cells and keeping the nervous system healthy, and is found in meat, fish, eggs and dairy. Sources for vegans are: breakfast cereals fortified with B12; other vegan products fortified with it (a lot of vegan milks are, for example, one glass a day of fortified soya milk provides the EU-recommended amount of Vitamin B12); and yeast extract, such as Marmite.

The other thing to be aware of is Omega-3 fatty acids, which can help maintain a healthy heart. These are found in chia seed, hemp seed and flax seed. I take care of it by adding a tablespoon of one of these to smoothies – but it is something to be conscious of.

A lot of people will ask you about iron, as the meat industry has done such a good marketing job in linking red meat with iron. It's actually the most common dietary deficiency in the world, so it's not specific to a vegan diet. In fact, a vegan diet can be very rich in iron. Good sources are: pulses, wholemeal bread, fortified breakfast cereals, dark green vegetables (like kale and broccoli), nuts and dried fruits. One thing to note is that plant-based iron can be harder for the body to absorb than the iron that comes from animal sources.

Additionally, tea and coffee can make it harder for your body to absorb iron, so you might want to avoid drinking these along with meals. On the other hand, vitamin C makes iron absorption easier. It's easy to sometimes combine a dose of vitamin C with your meal – it could be as easy as a glass of orange juice, or eating some fruit as dessert, or adding a few vitamin C sources like broccoli or cabbage to a stir fry.

If you want to research more about your dietary requirements (something everyone should do, regardless of diet), then the Vegan Society have an excellent app, 'VNutrition'.[27]

Surely honey is OK?

Honey is not vegan, it is created by bees and bees actually need honey to feed off in order to live. I personally don't want to mess with the bees; we need them *soooo* much more than they need us. They play such a vital part in crop pollination worldwide. And quite frankly, we have maple syrup, agave and even vegan honey which tastes the same. The bees can keep their honey in my opinion.

Isn't it better for the environment to eat locally reared meat than vegetables from all over the world?

Whilst of course it's preferable in many ways to eat local produce as much as possible, if you are focused on reducing your carbon footprint, what you eat is way more im-

"

If you are focused on reducing your carbon footprint, what you eat is way more important than where it's travelled from.

"

portant than where it's travelled from. Travel only counts for a very small proportion of a food's carbon footprint.[28]

Isn't a vegan diet really restrictive? What on earth do you eat?

I like to challenge people by pointing out how much of the food they already eat is vegan – and they like it! Beans on toast? Vegan. That packet of crisps on the way home? Vegan (depends a bit on flavour, but a lot of crisps are). Falafel wrap? Vegan. The fruit salad you had for dessert? Vegan.

If you take away the meat on your plate you may find that what remains is already vegan. You can eat *loads* as a vegan.

Humans are at the top of the food chain.

Just because we know *how* to kill animals does not mean we *should*. We can thrive on a plant-based diet; eating animal products is totally unnecessary for us to survive. Also we are not lions.

And there's this . . .

Eating vegan doesn't mean you *have* to be healthy. Although I would encourage it where possible, we all need to treat ourselves. Of course we all like our sugar fix and whilst you can get this from natural sources such

as fruits like dates, vegan sweets and chocolate do exist (halleluiah!) and they're just as good (if not better) than the non-vegan kind. Baked goods are not off limits either, along with junk food such as vegan burgers, pizzas etc. Basically anything you want, you can have vegan these days and you will not be disappointed with the taste as the technology is improving drastically every year. My favourites are vegan doughnuts from Crosstown or Beyond Meat burgers from Halo Burger. Vegan pizza is my Achilles heel and I actually love making my own.

Eating out

One thing you may realise when you start to eat out as a vegan is that the attitude you may be met with from staff is not always that welcoming. I would say that nine out of ten times I eat out (after careful planning of where I will go) I am met with helpful people who want to cater to my diet or already have an abundance of delicious options they can offer me. Then that other one time in ten, I get an awkward look and a slightly panicked human telling me they have nothing to offer. I have even been told (in a restaurant in Spain) that it would be impossible to make me a salad to eat and that it would be better if I left.

As a white privileged woman, I have rarely felt discriminated against. But that changed when I went vegan. I like to use situations like this as an opportunity to educate people where possible and I've definitely had to work on my tone of voice. But the ignorance and apathetic attitude of others will not hinder the way I choose to live and the cruelty-free world I am helping to build.

Another thing that may happen is that you will likely eat things here and there that are 'vegan' but actually contain milk or eggs. I've had quite a few occasions in hotels and restaurants (especially abroad where there may be a language barrier) where I have eaten something under the illusion that it was vegan and later found out that it was not. Normally it will be something like bread or pasta, as sometimes fresh pasta is cooked with egg, or in some countries a lot of bread has eggs in it. This can be disappointing, especially when you've done so much to avoid these kinds of products and you've committed to something that you think may be the right decision for you, for animals and for the planet.

It is quite literally impossible to be perfect.

The first few times this happened, I got really upset and down and felt guilty for not checking more thoroughly or not just avoiding something to be safe. I couldn't be more careful these days and it still happens! I now try not to let it get me down and I remember this kind of thing is bound to happen at some stage, especially when it's someone else making your food. I try to have the mindset of 'Well, I'm still making a conscious effort day-to-day and one little slip-up is not the end of the world'. Some people may take a more relaxed approach to this, which I think is also totally fine. We live in a very 'un-vegan' world and it is quite literally impossible to be perfect. Never forget that.

Here are a few cuisines you might encounter eating out, and how to navigate them as a vegan.

Indian food

With India having one of the lowest rates of meat consumption in the world, it's no wonder that Indian restaurants offer many delicious vegan meals that are part of this culinary tradition. Try chana masala (a chickpea curry), a daal (spiced lentils) or saag aloo (spinach and potato curry).

A few potential pitfalls to look out for: Indian food uses a lot of ghee (a kind of butter), so do ask if dishes contain that. Yoghurt is often used in Indian dips, so be careful to avoid.

Chinese food

Your best bet here is tofu – and most Chinese restaurants offer a delicious array of tofu dishes, cooked and flavoured differently. Menus will also feature fantastic vegetable sides; order a few to ensure you get a substantial meal.

Things to watch out for: the use of small amounts of egg in dishes, e.g. in egg-fried rice and stir fries. Small amounts of pork or prawns can sneak into things – do ask for clarity on the ingredients if you are unsure.

Thai food

Thai food is bursting with amazing flavours and textures. Go for creamy coconut Thai curries with tofu and vegetables; vegan pad thai; a spicy mango salad; or stir-fried vegetable dishes. Again, watch out for eggs (especially in a pad thai). Thai food often uses a dash of fish sauce for extra flavour, so ensure you specify you don't eat that.

Fish and chips

OK, so you're obviously not going to be able to eat the fish, but fish and chip shops are increasingly offering vegan alternatives – and these are also finding their way onto pub menus across the country.[29]

One thing to check before you buy a portion of chips is what they have been fried in, as some places still fry in beef dripping, not vegetable oil.

Italian food

Italian restaurants can be a bit trickier, as so many of the staple Italian foods we see in the UK are pizza and pastas, often featuring a lot of cheese. Many restaurants are now offering vegan options, but it's by no means universal. Check out tomato-based pasta sauces, making sure they don't contain anchovies. A good option can again be starters and sides, such as bruschetta. Most dried pasta is vegan, but fresh pasta can contain egg, so do check.

Getting creative

It can be really disheartening when there is nothing vegan on the menu. If this is the case, look for what might be adaptable – can the cheese be left off a dish, for example? Or see what sides are vegan – salads, vegetables (check if they are cooked in butter), chips, bread – and order these to make up a meal. It might not be the most amazing dinner of your life, but you should be able to pull something together. Do – politely! – let the restaurant know of your disappointment. You're a paying customer and they should be able to accommodate your dietary requests.

You can use an app called 'Happy Cow' to check for vegan restaurants close to you – it's also invaluable for travelling.

Alcohol

Animal products may be used in the production of alcoholic drinks, such as isinglass (which is made from the swim bladders of fish), egg whites or gelatine. Animal products, such as cochineal, may also be used to colour drinks. To check, go to barnivore.com, which maintains a comprehensive database of what alcoholic brands are vegan or not.

Hidden nasties

Food labelling can be confusing at the best of times, and it can also hide some animal ingredients. Your safest bet is to buy foods labelled with the Vegan Society sunflower trademark, but not all vegan products will have this yet, so you might end up doing some label checking of your own. Supermarkets are getting better at being clear if their own brands are vegan or not, and I'd encourage you to contact any suppliers where this is unclear. Brands respond to consumer pressure, so do ask the question.

Check out anything bold in the ingredients; these are often common allergens but will include milk and eggs, for example.

A good tip is to check out the 'free from' aisle in supermarkets. This is where you'll often find things like dairy-free pesto, for example, as well as dairy-free chocolate and other goodies. These won't necessarily be vegan, but you can often find a lot of 'accidentally' vegan products in this aisle. You can also use an app like 'Is it Vegan?' to check products easily on your phone.

When you're checking labels, here are a list of common animal-derived ingredients to look out for.

E Number	What is it?	Uses	Action to take
E120	Cochineal (another name for carminic acid, a pigment taken from the abdomen)	Food colouring and cosmetics	Avoid
E322	Lecithin (can be made from soya or, less commonly, from eggs)	Emulsifier used in wide range of foods	Check the label for the Vegan Trademark or contact supplier
E422	Glycerol (is mainly plant-based but there are still instances of it being derived from animal fat)	Sweetener and solvent used in wide range of foods, beverages and cosmetics	Check the label for the Vegan Trademark or contact supplier
E542	Edible Bone Phosphate (a product made from the bones of cattle or pigs)	Cosmetics, toothpaste, nutritional supplement and anti-caking agent	Avoid
E631	Disodium Inosinate (can be produced from meat, fish or tapioca starch)	Flavour enhancer often found in snack foods	Check the label for the Vegan Trademark or contact supplier
E901	Beeswax	Glazing agent, candles, confectionery, cosmetics like moisturisers or lip products	Avoid
E904	Shellac (derived from the lac beetle)	Furniture polish, glazing agents, confectionery	Avoid
E471	Mono and di-glycerides of fatty acids (sometimes derived from animal fats)	Crisps, bread, dairy-free spread	Check the label for the Vegan Trademark or contact supplier
E920	An amino acid, also known as L-Cysteine	Bread, biscuits, wraps	Check the label for the Vegan Trademark or contact supplier

Recipes

It can be tricky to know where to start when it comes to eating a balanced, vegan diet. Here are some of my favourite recipes to make sure you're getting all the nutrients you need.

Tofu and Cabbage Stir fry

1 tbsp coconut oil or light olive oil
1 red pepper, sliced
Half a block of firm tofu, cut into cubes
1 courgette chopped into small pieces
3 cloves garlic, finely chopped
Half a head of cabbage, shredded
2 tbsp liquid aminos
1 tbsp sesame oil
1 tsp ground ginger

Heat a frying pan on a medium heat with a tbsp of light olive oil/coconut oil. Add the red pepper along with the tofu, courgette and garlic. Fry for 2 – 3 mins, stirring occasionally until slightly brown.

Then add the cabbage followed by 50ml of filtered water. Allow to simmer for a few minutes and then add the liquid aminos, sesame oil and ginger and stir in together evenly.

Cook for a further few minutes or until the cabbage has wilted and serve on its own or with brown rice/quinoa. Season with salt and pepper.

Cauliflower 'Cheese'

1 cup cashews, soaked for an hour (or 30 minutes in boiling water)
1 head of cauliflower, cut into florets
1 head of broccoli, cut into florets
250ml stock
500ml plant milk
3 tbsps nutritional yeast
half tsp garlic granules
2 tbsp Dijon mustard
juice of 1 lemon
2 tbsp plain flour

Topping:
1 cup dried breadcrumbs
2 tbsp melted vegan butter
1 tsp garlic granules

Heat your oven to 200 degrees celsius. Boil or steam your cauliflower & broccoli for around 3 minutes and set to one side.

Drain the cashews and blend them with the stock, plant milk, nutritional yeast, garlic granules, mustard and lemon.

Once smooth add to a large saucepan and stir in your flour on a medium heat. Once the sauce has thickened remove it from the heat. Pour half the sauce into a medium sized dish. Add your cooked broccoli & cauliflower to the dish and pour over the remaining sauce. Combine the topping ingredients and evenly spread over the top of the sauce. Cook in the oven for 20-30 mins or until the topping goes brown and crispy.

Chickpea Chuna Melt

1 400g can chickpeas (drained)
Zest and juice of ½ lemon
60g vegan mayonnaise
1 tsp sweet miso
1 tsp Dijon mustard (optional)
1 tbsp nutritional yeast
salt and pepper
1 tbsp capers
ciabatta bread sliced
vegan cheese sliced

Combine all the filling ingredients except the capers and blend on a high speed. If you don't have a high-speed blender you can mash the chickpeas with a fork and then stir in the remaining ingredients. Mix in the capers and spread evenly onto the ciabatta. Add 1 – 2 slices of vegan cheese (I recommend Violife) and toast in your toastie maker, if you have one. If you don't have one, toast the bread, then add the cheese and heat under the grill for 1 minute and then add the filling.

Greek Salad

1 cucumber, sliced
1 cup cherry tomatoes, sliced
25g pitted olives
½ small red onion, sliced
half a block of tofu, cubed
2 tbsp olive oil
2 tbsp balsamic glaze
1 tsp oregano
salt and pepper

Add the cucumber, tomatoes, olives and onion to a bowl. Combine the balsamic glaze, olive oil and oregano. Pour half over the cubed tofu in a separate bowl, and mix. Add the tofu to the salad and pour over the rest of the dressing and combine. Add salt and pepper.

Cashew 'Cheese'

1 cup cashews in boiling water for 30 minutes
2 tbsp nutritional yeast
1 tsp mustard
1 tsp smoked paprika
1 tsp garlic powder
juice of half a lemon
1 tsp apple cider vinegar
salt and pepper

Blend all the ingredients until smooth, using the cashew water. You can add more boiling water to alter the thickness.

Butternut Squash Curry

2 tbsp olive oil
2 cloves garlic chopped
1 small butternut squash, peeled and diced
6 new potatoes, halved
50g mushrooms, chopped
curry powder 1 tbsp
1 tbsp ginger
½ tsp cinnamon
1 small green chilli, chopped finely
1 can coconut milk
½ can chopped tomatoes

Add the olive oil to the pan along with the garlic, butternut squash and potatoes. Cook on a medium heat until the garlic has browned slightly. Then add the mushrooms, followed by the curry powder, ginger, cinnamon and chili. Stir and cook for two minutes. Then add the coconut milk and chopped tomatoes. Allow to simmer for ten minutes or until the potatoes and butternut squash have gone soft. Season with salt and pepper and serve alone or with rice.

Sweet and Sour Tofu

200g firm tofu, cubed
1 tbsp soy sauce
½ tsp garlic powder
40g cornstarch
20g vegetable oil

Sauce:
50g brown sugar
20g ketchup
20ml rice vinegar
20ml water
1 tbsp liquid aminos
½ red pepper chopped
½ green pepper chopped
20g pineapple, chopped (optional)
1 tbsp sesame seeds (garnish)

Add the tofu to a bowl and combine with the soy sauce, garlic powder and cornstarch. Make sure the tofu is covered evenly and then fry in a shallow pan with the vegetable oil on a medium heat until crispy (around 6 minutes). Then add the peppers and pineapple and fry for around 4-5 minutes or until the peppers are browned slightly. Whisk the rest of the sauce ingredients in a separate bowl and pour over the tofu and veg. stir to combine. Simmer for roughly 4 mins. Remove from heat and eat with rice or noodles, feel free to add other vegetables like broccoli. Top with sesame seeds, salt and pepper.

American Style Pancakes

125g plain flour
1 tbsp baking powder
240ml soya milk (or plant milk of choice)
1 tsp vanilla extract
1 tsp vegan butter

Combine all the ingredients in a bowl with a whisk. Add a knob of vegan butter to a frying pan on a medium heat. Use a tablespoon/ladle to add the mixture to the pan and fry until you begin to see little bubbles and then flip over. Serve with vegan butter and maple syrup or toppings of your choice.

Healthy Vegan Brownies

3 ripe bananas
60g cocoa powder
120g smooth peanut butter/almond butter
handful of chopped pistachios

It's essential you use ripe bananas for this, the browner the better. Mash them with a fork and add the cocoa powder and nut butter, you can blend the ingredients together to get a smoother finish or combine with a whisk.

Pour the mixture into a baking tray (lined with greasproof paper) and top with the pistachios. Bake for 20 mins at 160 celsius. Remove and leave to cool for ten minutes before slicing.

Salted Caramel and Raspberry Protein Shake

1 frozen banana
handful frozen raspberries
1 scoop salted caramel vegan protein powder
100 ml soya milk
1 tbsp flaxseed
handful of ice

Blend all the ingredients together, add water to reduce thickness.

Clothing

For centuries humans have worn animal skins and furs as a form of clothing. Long before fashion, this was a necessary means to protect humans from intense cold and harsh sunshine. As humans adapted, so did their tools and they managed to find ways to cut and shape skins to form clothing that would protect them from weather the majority of the time. Of course their technology was nowhere near as advanced as it is today; they were working with raw materials and basic tools. When animal farming began, they would also have used wool from sheep to make yarn. But the truth is, had our ancestors not used those animals products to wear back then it is unlikely humans would have survived.

Today, in many parts of the world, the situation is completely different. We wear clothes to look and feel good, with an abundance of choice available. Individual style is important – who doesn't want to look good and express themselves via their clothing? – but it's not worth the suffering of animals. Now we know that we can use plant fibres to form clothing and a huge variety of it! Unfortunately, the use of animal products in clothing is still rife, and an update in attitudes is long overdue.

Fur

The use of fur is frowned upon in most parts of the world, with fur farming being banned in many countries such as Austria, Belgium and the United Kingdom. California was the first state in America to ban the sale of fur and in 2018 the UK banned fur from Fashion Week, which was a huge step in the right direction and a campaign I had worked closely on.

Most people know how cruel fur is, and whether they're vegan or not a lot of people would be against wearing or buying fur. Why? Well there are a few reasons:

- The production of fur involves the capture of wild animals, such as coyotes, in leg traps where they suffer until found and killed.

- There are thousands of fur farms all over the world. Around one hundred million animals, such as foxes, rabbits and raccoon dogs, are bred in tiny wire cages where they will spend their entire lives until killed and skinned for their fur. The killing of these animals involves gassing, electrocuting and sometimes even beating to death.

I believe the use of fur has reduced due to the bad publicity it has received. With many high-profile celebrities doing anti-fur campaigns, it has become less and less 'cool' to be seen wearing real animal fur. It has also got to a point where the people who do still wear fur are in a minority and as the saying goes, 'majority rules' – people like to follow the trend and thank goodness for that in this case.

Faux fur is not only more ethical, but it is also less harmful to the environment, contrary to popular belief. Fur factory pollution is a big environmental issue caused by disease and waste from animals. The animal waste contains high concentrations of nitrogen and phosphorus, which are considered among the most common forms of water pollution. Ammonia from fur farms has been shown to cause damage to forests by affecting trees and other vegetation directly as well as indirectly via forest soils. Not only do these farms affect the environment negatively, they are also a risk to the health of wildlife and even humans due to the transmission of viral and bacterial diseases, fungal infections and even parasites.

The chemical treatment of fur is also a huge issue. Two of the main methods of dressing fur skins involve the use of toxic and carcinogenic chemicals, which are incidentally highly dangerous to human health. Independent research

has shown that these chemicals can linger on the fur trims on children's fashion wear.[30]

While faux fur made from acrylics and plastics is not necessarily environmentally friendly, there are a lot of brands that make sustainable faux fur from recycled and/or natural materials. These eco-friendly alternatives are not only fashionable and warm, but they are definitely the cruelty-free alternative that needs to be considered by everyone. A lot of vegans are conscious of their impact on the planet (and of course animals), but this is also the case for non-vegans.

The changing attitude to fur actually gives me hope. For our grandparents' generation, fur was seen as an incredible luxury – something to be coveted. Just think how attitudes have changed. I think that many people who still buy fur don't really understand what they are buying. They might be buying into a brand they like or a style that they want, without knowing the reality. This is why education is so important. There is always a cruelty-free alternative and it's important to check the label.

Recently, there has been a growing trend for small amounts of fur, eg trims on parkas and on bobble hats. Again, I think a lot of people don't realise where this is coming from. That cute fluffy pompom is often raccoon fur. Make sure it's fake.

Leather

Much like fur, leather is another animal product that dates back for centuries and is also the cause of harm to millions of animals. When I went vegan, I thought it was fine to continue wearing leather as leather, in my opinion, was not the cause of death of an animal. I believed it to be a by-product of the meat industry and that me not buying it would make no difference at all. I got called a hypocrite by a lot of people in the beginning of my journey and it wasn't until I researched the topic that I began to understand why.

For a long time, leather has been seen as both an essential and a luxury item. We use it for shoes, bags, clothes, furniture and even cars. We're conditioned into thinking it's the best possible option – natural, durable and beautiful.

But where does it come from? Every year the global leather industry kills more than a billion animals including cows and their calves, pigs, sheep, ostriches, snakes, kangaroos, alligators and more. But what people don't realise is that a lot of leather can also come from animals like dogs and cats. Most of the raw leather materials originate from India or China, where the animals are kept in horrific conditions and welfare laws are amiss. A huge portion of animals killed for meat also have their skins sold for leather, but there are millions of animals being raised in these countries purely for their skins. The demand for leather products is so big now, you can hardly differentiate between those animals being raised for meat and those being raised for their skin.

When you own a leather product, it can be impossible to tell what it is made from and where is was made, because the country that is stated is normally the country where the product was designed or manufactured, not where the animal was raised and slaughtered for the raw ma-

"

When you own a leather
product, it can be impossible
to tell what it is made from
and where is was made.

"

terial. With welfare laws being very different in less developed countries, it is very possible that the animal will have been skinned alive.

" Leather is neither a sustainable nor an ethical option. "

For those that care about the environment, the production of leather creates harmful waste due to the use of chemicals in tanneries and the amount of waste that comes off the skins. After usage, the water waste containing these chemicals is often just dumped on fields or in rivers. In many developing countries this has caused extremely bad water pollution in areas near tanneries. The chemicals are not only bad for the environment and wild animals, but also for humans, as in some countries water from these polluted rivers is the main source of drinking water for the local population. Not to mention the amount of land and water that are used to raise the animals that are then killed for their skins.

Leather is neither a sustainable nor an ethical option and these days we have so many other options to choose from. If you buy vegan and sustainable leather you will not only be helping the animals but the environment too!

It can be tough to throw away your leather goods, especially when you have spent a lot of money on them. You don't have to do this and you don't have to feel bad if you don't! Once you've made the decision to live a vegan lifestyle, it's the decisions you make moving forward that are the ones the make all the difference.

Aren't natural products better, as they are biodegradable?

This is a very common misconception. Think about it: leather and fur have to be treated, otherwise they would rot in your wardrobe! As mentioned above, this process involves many toxic chemicals, and leather treated this way consequently takes twenty-five to fifty years to break down (the same as a polystyrene cup)[31].

I will also add, though, that not all vegan materials are created equal. There are legitimate concerns about PVC and PU, and the environmental footprint of these materials. We should all be mindful of what we buy, thinking about how often we will wear it and the materials it's made from.

There are loads of vegan alternatives to PVC or PU: organic cotton, linen, bamboo, tencel, to name just a few. More and more companies are researching amazing fabrics with sustainable properties. Look out for Piñatex (which is made from pineapple leaf fibre), or MuSkin (a vegan leather made from mushrooms). You might already

be familiar with Lyocell and Modal, which are fibres manufactured from wood pulp.

When it comes to vegan clothing, I tend to just buy vegan items from standard clothing shops, not go to specialist vegan clothing brands (although these are really starting to take off and offer a lot more variety than before). Check the labels – watch out for wool mix fabrics, for example, or horn buttons on clothing, and where possible invest in sustainable materials.

Trainers

Even if you opt for a synthetic trainer, they can be constructed using animal-derived materials such as glue (made from animal bones) or certain dyes. The best thing is to check with the manufacturer – most likely some styles will be vegan, and others not.

What about other animal products?

There are many other animal products that are used for clothing, including wool, silk and feathers. When I chose to live a vegan lifestyle I was choosing to recognise that animals are not commodities. When animals are being raised because they have a certain 'use' that can be exploited, this means taking away their freedom, their happiness and, a lot of the time, their safety.

While some people may think sheep need to be sheared, this is only necessary because certain sheep have been genetically bred to a point where they produce more wool than necessary. Others are sheared too early, as leaving them to shed naturally would mean a loss in profits due to the seasons. Sheep have holes punched into their ears so they can be numbered, they have their tails cut off and they are also castrated from a young age. A lot of these procedures happen without anaesthesia, and if that isn't something you would want done to yourself, why should it be done to them?

Feathers are used not only for clothing but also for bedding and furniture. Ducks and geese have their feathers plucked from them while they are still alive; sometimes they die from the shock and pain. If they don't die, farmers will allow them to grow their feathers back and the process will be repeated. We now have synthetic bedding and feathers, which are a much kinder alternative.

And in case you didn't know, because this is something I found out years after going vegan, silk worms are boiled alive to create silk. Not so luxurious-sounding.

We don't *need* to use animals to dress nicely or to keep warm. New vegan brands are coming out every year and we are constantly finding sustainable vegan options for clothing alternatives to animal products. You may not be in a position to give this up all at once and that is fine. But, the less we buy these products, the less these creatures will be used and abused by us. The future is bright and less tainted with death: let's move towards that together at whatever reasonable pace works for us.

Is it OK to wear vintage fur or leather?

For me, no. Vintage clothing is a very ethical choice when it comes to environmental footprint, but as a vegan, I wouldn't *want* to wear animal skins.

If I wear real fur or leather, I am advertising that product and potentially creating demand. I also think there is a risk of keeping a trend going: if you look amazing in a vintage fur-trimmed coat, other people are going to seek out the same thing, and demand will go up again. The same is true of vintage bags, which are often made of exotic animal skins.

Vegans don't use animals, full stop. If I wear leather or fur, even if it's vintage, that confuses the overall message of what veganism is about. Equally, if I wear vegan leather or fur, I always do my best to point it out where possible. I always tag faux fur on posts where I'm wearing it as I would hate for people to think otherwise and sometimes they can look the same.

Lifestyle

Once you've become vegan in your diet and clothing, you can start to consider changes elsewhere in your life. A major one I am often asked about is beauty and make-up. We use these products every day, and want to feel good, so it's important to make sure we are living vegan in this respect as well. The good news is there is an abundance of amazing products out there.

Skin care and beauty

From a young age, I have been aware of animal testing in cosmetics. Much like the anti-fur movement, I think this is thanks to huge animal charities such as PETA getting animal testing a lot of press over the years with huge campaigns normally involving naked celebrities (it gets people's attention!).

Animal testing involves many animals such as rabbits, mice, rats, dogs, cats and monkeys. They are kept in labs and have products or medicines squirted and injected into their skin or eyeballs amongst other things. In 2013 the EU banned the testing of animals for cosmetic purposes, but unfortunately the issue is far from solved. Cosmetics companies all around the world are still testing on animals. Why? Because they want to be a part of the Chinese market where animal testing is required by law.

A cruelty-free company does not test their products or ingredients on animals. Period. A lot of companies will say that they don't test 'unless required to by law', i.e. in China. These companies are not 'required' to sell in China and therefore have no excuse to be testing on animals. It's just pure greed, if you ask me.

Plus there are *soooo* many incredible and wonderful brands that are cruelty free and proud (so they should be). If you want to be sure a product is cruelty free, check for the leaping bunny logo. Leaping Bunny also run a directory on their website and have an app, which you can use to look up brands to check whether they are cruelty free.

It is possible to have a cruelty-free brand that doesn't have vegan make-up, and it is also possible for a vegan skincare or beauty brand to test on animals and therefore not, I repeat *not*, be cruelty free. It's important to be aware of this complexity, so you can make an informed choice about what you're buying.

There are many ingredients involved with beauty that are not vegan. Here are the main ones to be aware of:

- Carmine/carminic acid/cochineal: crushed insects are used to form a deep red colour, often used in lipsticks.

- Beeswax/cera alba: this can be used in lip balms, lipsticks and skin care.

- Honey: can be used in a variety of skincare products, including face masks.

- Lanolin: derived from sheep wool, often used in lip products.

- Shellac: obtained by killing lac bugs and often used in nail and hair products.

- Glycerin: generally from animal fats although there are plant-based alternatives; used in many different skincare products, from moisturisers to serums.

- Casein/sodium caseinate/caseinate: derived from cows' milk although plant based alternatives are possible; can be found in a range of cosmetics, hair treatments and beauty masks.

- Animal hair: often used in make-up brushes and fake eyelashes; synthetic alternatives are not only easier to clean but also softer (in my opinion).

- Collagen: derived from animal tissue, bone, skin or ligaments of cows or other animals. Plant-based alternatives include soya protein and almond oil. Found in face creams, and sometimes in oral beauty supplements.

- Keratin: from the hair and horns of animals; used in hair and nail strengthening products. Vegan soya protein and almond oil are used.

Watch out for new products coming on the market, such as the use of snail mucus, which has been a real trend lately, particularly in sheet masks and K-beauty.

I've been buying vegan and cruelty-free make-up for years. Many of the most 'well known' brands are cruelty free and have an array of vegan options. Just make sure you check the packaging and if in doubt, don't buy. I don't think it will be too long before animal testing on cosmetics is banned worldwide, but it takes people avoiding those products and companies to make a difference. Power to the people.

Some of my favourite make-up brands:

- Cover FX
- Kat Von D
- Hourglass
- Milk Make up
- Tarte
- Too Faced
- Lime Crime
- The Body Shop
- Illamasqua
- Bare minerals

For skin care:

- Lisa Franklin UK
- Pai Skin Care
- Dermalogica
- Rodial
- Herbivore
- Botanicals
- Lush cosmetics
- Skyn ICELAND
- Deciem
- Face Theory

Pets, or as I like to call them, fluffy companions

Animals bring so much joy to our lives, but having a pet does bring up important issues in relation to veganism. Firstly, there is the ethical question of keeping an animal with you – you are, after all, subjecting them to your life and your routines, instead of them being free. For me, this translates as a responsibility to look after animals as best you possibly can. It also means not using animals as a commodity – by which I mean, avoiding puppy farms and certain fashionable breeds. Breeding is cruel, especially involving puppy farms, where dogs are intensively bred and kept in awful conditions, and puppies separated from their mothers before they are ready, purely for profit. These puppy farms can exist in the UK, or elsewhere in the world, with puppies sold and transported. For me, this goes against vegan principles.

Humans have bred some types of dog to have exaggerated features. While these might look 'cute' to some people, these features lead to serious health problems and suffering for the dogs. For example, pugs with their flattened faces often have severe breathing difficulties and eye problems, with painful surgeries the only option to help them. Many vets are now calling for people to avoid these breeds.

If you are considering a dog, I would urge you not to support this commoditisation of animals by buying a specific breed. Instead, choose a rescue dog – my own dogs (and cat!) are rescues, and they are the most wonderful companions. You're giving an animal that already exists a second chance in life, and that is the most ethical option.

Charities that do amazing work include:

Many Tears Rescue

Battersea

Dogs Trust UK

RSCPA

Blue Cross rescue

What do you feed your pets?

This is one of the questions I get asked all the time, and it can pose a real ethical dilemma for vegans. If you are eliminating animal products from your life, it will of course feel very wrong to be buying them to feed your pets.

I've done a lot of research into this, and it *is* possible to feed dogs a vegan diet and for them to thrive on it, as the digestive system of domestic dogs is so different to that of their wild ancestors. I make food for my dogs – so much commercial pet food is made up of the grossest by-products of the meat production industry. We would never expect humans to eat this, so why expect our animal companions to do so?

It's very important to note that every dog will have different dietary requirements. You should seek veterinary advice to help transition a dog to a vegan diet and monitor how they are getting along with it.

I do share what I feed my dogs on Instagram from time to time. A recipe might look something like this:

Sweet potatoes, boiled – if you leave the skin on, it needs to be blended very well after you've cooked it. If you don't have a powerful blender, take the skin off. It can upset dogs' stomachs otherwise.

Quinoa (well-cooked). To vary things, I might also add beans, lentils or chickpeas – again these need to be blended very well, otherwise they can cause tummy troubles.

Add some vegetables, again checking carefully what is suitable for dogs. I often use broccoli or spinach. Don't add too many veggies; they can be too fibrous.

I then add:

- A tablespoon of flax seed.

- A tablespoon of apple cider vinegar – this can be brilliant for soothing stomachs if they get gassy (works just as well for humans as dogs, by the way).

- Hemp oil.

- Nutritional yeast.

Then add lots of water and blend everything together. You can also get vegan dried dog food, made from soy, that can help balance your dog's nutritional needs. Check out V-dog, Ami, Benevo, Pet Guard and Wysong Vegan.

When it comes to cats, there is less research available and cats are obligate carnivores – they rely on taurine (an animal-derived product) to survive. However, just like we supplement B12 it is possible to find vegan cat food with synthetic taurine. I know people with very healthy vegan cats (some have cured skin issues through feeding them

vegan diets) but I'm not saying it's for everyone and it is something you should think about before getting a cat as they may not be able to survive on a vegan diet. I have recently started to feed my cats a vegan dry food since finding out about the terrible quality ingredients found in some cat food and how this can contribute to poor health. I want my animals to live a long and healthy life and that's why I feed them vegan food. So far, so good. If their health was ever to deteriorate, I would of course re-evaluate this. I have no problem with feeding my cats meat if that is what they need, but right now they are healthy.

Entertainment and sport

Sadly, there is a long history of animals being used for our amusement. Hunting might once have been essential to our survival, but in many countries it now continues as a sport. In the UK, hunting, shooting and deer stalking are still ongoing, but primarily as 'sports'.

In other countries around the world wild animals are hunted for their skin, horns or tusks. Elephants and rhinos are nearing extinction. They are hunted and killed for their horns and tusks and although these are illegal to sell and buy, they are still extremely valuable on the black market, with rhino horn being thought to have medicinal benefits.

Trophy hunting is another so-called sport that has caused controversy around the world, with many believing it is cruel and wrong. The motivation of a trophy hunter is to gain parts of a rare or exotic animal for display and bragging rights. Animals involved in this 'sport' involve bears, wolves, elephants and zebra. I have found it interesting over the years when I meet people who are opposed to the killing of exotic animals to the point where it may bring them to tears, yet have little to no compassion towards the animals that they eat. If you are reading this and that may apply to you, ask yourself this: what rights do those animals have above the ones killed for food? And if your answer is conservation-based reasoning, then you are already in agreement with veganism, as animal agriculture is the leading cause of species extinction around the world, with hundreds of thousands of acres of rainforest being destroyed every year to make room for livestock.

There are many other 'sports' around the world that involve cruelty to animals, such as bull fighting (which is also considered an 'art'), rodeo (cowboys attempt to bring bucking horses under control, or rope young calves and drag them to the ground), cock fighting (where cocks are bred in dreadful conditions and mistreated to make them bad tempered), dog fighting and horse racing (to name a few). Some may not agree that horse racing is cruel, but unfortunately these horses are risking their lives without being given a choice and many die each year. Regardless of that, race horses who become 'unfit to race' will usually be slaughtered. All too often in greyhound racing, the dogs spend most of their time in small kennels, unable to socialise, and many don't receive adequate health care. The racing itself is cruel and dangerous, with multiple injuries occurring during races, and many dogs put down when they are deemed no longer suitable for the track. Yet many people still see dog racing as a harmless night out[32]. Please, please don't attend events like these, and tell your friends the truth about what happens.

"

We don't need to abuse animals for entertainment.

"

You could also campaign for an end to these kinds of cruel sports, by writing to your MP or signing petitions. We don't need to abuse animals for entertainment.

Travel

I have some horror stories from when I first travelled out of the UK as a vegan. One of my first trips was to Greece and the team in the hotel I was staying in had zero vegan options but very kindly (and ambitiously) offered to veganise any option on their menu for me – stuffed ravioli, pasta sauces, chocolate mousse etc.

I later realised, towards the end of the trip, that they hadn't been doing this at all and in fact they had been feeding me their normal menu dishes and lying about what was inside. I was furious and felt disgusted by what they had done. If my dietary requirement had been due to religious purposes or an allergy then it would have been treated as a very different situation. It was that day that I realised it was possible to be discriminated against just because you didn't want to eat food that had animal products in it.

This was a while ago now and I think we have advanced our knowledge globally about what veganism is and how to cater for it. And travelling as a vegan *can* be super easy, but it totally depends on where you are travelling to. I always research the culture of the place I am going to and see how familiar it is with veganism.

I tend to check the restaurants in the local area using the 'Happy Cow' app. This is an app that you can use to see which restaurants nearby have vegan options; alternatively you can type in a location you will be going to and check there. The Vegan Society also have a 'Vegan Passport' app you can use, that explains what you do and don't eat in a variety of languages, to help with communication.

I also like to check the menu for the hotel I would like to be staying in and see if they offer vegan options. I usually choose a hotel based on this detail, amongst other necessities. If a hotel has one or two vegan options on the breakfast and/or lunch menu, this is great and I will normally be more inclined to stay there. Sometimes the hotel I am staying at is chosen on my behalf due to work; however, I am lucky that I can usually have a large influence over this although I imagine a lot of people will not have that luxury. In this case, communication with the hotel is key. I like to email them in advance (email can usually work better if there is a language barrier) and just explain my dietary requirements in a polite manner:

'To Whom It May Concern,

I am very much looking forward to my stay with you on (said date). I would like to inform you that I follow a strict vegan diet. Would you be able to kindly let me know what kind of food you would be able to offer during my stay?

Many thanks in advance.

Best wishes,
Lucy'

Something to this nature will give the team a heads-up in order for them to prepare some options that will be readily available to you when you stay with them. I actually think most hotels would be grateful for the advance warning.

There are of course times when I have arrived at a hotel and they have acted completely clueless (which maybe they are) about any conversations that have happened prior to my stay. In situations like this I do have a few staple meals that will normally be accessible in most places.

Breakfast

- Toast with either avocado (and tomato) or peanut butter and/or banana. You will need to check the bread is vegan, as in a lot of countries, it is not. Just last year I went to a supermarket local to where I was staying and bought a loaf of vegan-friendly bread to bring down to breakfast with me in the mornings. Sometimes you have to get creative!

- Porridge with soya milk. Most places will have oats and some kind of milk alternative so this a really easy alternative.

- Fresh fruit platter.

- Breakfast smoothie without honey or milk.

Lunch/dinner

- If there is a salad bar then that's always great as you can literally make your own salad (I sometimes like to add chips as a side). Most restaurants will be able to whip you up a vegan salad whether it's tomato and avocado or a Greek salad without the cheese!

- Pasta. Again, most hotels will have a vegan pasta option. Most dried pasta is vegan; fresh pasta is usually not so be sure to check. Then it's normally easy to have it with a fresh tomato sauce and maybe even some cooked veggies or garlic.

- There may be dishes on the menu that you can help them to veganise. Risotto, for instance – can this be cooked with veggie stock instead of cream? And for vegetarian dishes containing cheese or eggs I would always ask if there is a way they can do it without; seven out of ten times they can.

Self-catering

If you happen to be staying in a self-service apartment or villa this can actually be easier a lot of the time, especially if you're not opposed to cooking!

Now if you're staying somewhere like LA or Sydney, you will be able to go to Whole Food or a supermarket and pick up vegan-friendly ready meals. LA is the dream place if you are vegan, that city is so ahead of the game. Amsterdam is also amazing! I've heard great things about Tel Aviv too.

In other cultures, veganism might not be quite so well understood. That means going back to cooking with staple foods, like veg, rice, pasta, beans, pulses etc. For instance, I regularly travel to Barbados with my boyfriend and his family. There are hardly any vegan restaurants on the island, except one or two (which are great) and I spend most of my time cooking.

Opposite are some easy options I use as go-tos when I am in a situation like this.

Tourist attractions on holiday

Sadly, many destinations feature the exploitation of animals. From zoos to sealife parks, local festivals that might involve animal cruelty, tourist traps like 'tiger temples' where animals are drugged so tourists can pose with them, or elephant camps – it pays to be aware of what attractions you visit on holiday. I am against anything where animals are being exploited in unnatural conditions for commercial gain.

'If you can ride, hug, or take a selfie with a wild animal, chances are the venue is cruel. Don't go!'
World Animal Protection

Self-catering go-to options

- Salad.

- Veggie wrap.

- Three-bean chilli.

- Roasted veg and baked tofu.

- Stir-fried veg with rice noodles.

- Soup.

- Baked sweet potato with chilli and hummus.

- Pasta with veg and tomato sauce.

- Steamed greens with quinoa and garlic.

- Homemade nut milk.

This organisation has a very helpful guide you can download on their website (worldanimalprotection.org) about how to be animal friendly on holiday. It also does excellent campaigning work you could get involved in, such as pressuring Tripadvisor to stop promoting cruel tourist attractions.

Choose to lend your support to organisations that support genuine conservation work in the wild.

When it comes to buying souvenirs, be aware of animal ingredients, such as horn, leather or coral (particularly used in jewellery).

BON VOYAGE

Boutique Hotels for the Conscious Traveler

Conclusion

'm sure the journey you've just been on having read this book has been relatively intense and perhaps even a bit of a shock to the system. That's OK. It's a lot to take in and it can be tricky to revaluate pretty much everything you do day-to-day. One word of advice – take it at your own pace. Only you know that and only you know what is doable.

I will also say this, I'm writing this book in 2020, I know that I haven't covered everything. Although there is a lot that I have learnt, I realise the learning isn't going to stop anytime soon. Each person's journey and experience in life will be totally unique to them and there's something quite beautiful about that. What's important is that we continue to evolve and work together to make this world a better place for us *and* the animals we share it with. It's not always easy going against the grain of the world or standing up for what you think is right, but sooner or later I truly believe this 'lifestyle' will be the norm and you're about to help shape the world. The efforts of every person, whether they are big or small, matter. Enjoy this journey!

Endnotes

1   Vegan Society, 'Definition of veganism', vegansociety.com. https://www.vegansociety.com/go-vegan/definition-veganism

2   Vegan Society (2014) Ripened by Human Determination, vegansociety.com. https://www.vegansociety.com/sites/default/files/uploads/Ripened%20by%20human%20determination.pdf

3   Sarah Griffiths, 'Why fish do not deserve their reputation for forgetfulness', bbc.co.uk, 17 April 2017. http://www.bbc.com/earth/story/20170426-why-fish-do-not-deserve-their-reputation-for-forgetfulness

4   Lori Marino and Christina M. Colvin, 'Thinking Pigs: Cognition, Emotion, and Personality', The Humane Society Institute for Science and Policy, 2016. https://animalstudiesrepository.org/cgi/viewcontent.cgi?article=1000&context=mammal

5   Zachary Toliver, 'Six Olympic Champions You Probably Had No Clue Were Vegan', peta.org, February 13 2019. https://www.peta.org/blog/6-olympic-champions-probably-no-clue-vegan/

6   Cahul Milmo, Alexandra Heal and Andrew Wasley, 'Revealed: Heavy toll of injury suffered by slaughter workers serving Britain's £8bn meat industry'. inews.co.uk, 29 July 2018. https://inews.co.uk/news/uk/revealed-heavy-toll-of-injury-and-amputations-suffered-by-slaughter-workers-serving-britains-8bn-meat-industry-180819. https://metro.co.uk/2017/12/31/how-killing-animals-everyday-leaves-slaughterhouse-workers-traumatised-7175087/

7   Evelyn Medawar, Sebastian Huhn, Arno Villringer & A. Veronica Witte, 'The effects of plant-based diets on the body and the brain: a systematic review', 12 September 2019.   https://www.nature.com/articles/s41398-019-0552-0

8   Harvard School of Public Health, 'The nutrition source: Vegetables and fruits', hsph.harvard.edu. https://www.hsph.harvard.edu/nutritionsource/what-should-you-eat/vegetables-and-fruits/

9   Guy Hajj Boutros, Marie-Anne Landry-Duval, Mauricio Garzon and Anthony D. Karelis, 'Is a vegan diet detrimental to endurance and muscle strength?', nature.com, 24 April 2020. https://www.nature.com/articles/s41430-020-0639-y

10   John Vidal, '"Tip of the iceberg": Is our destruction of nature responsible for Covid-19?', theguardian.com, 18 March 2020. https://www.theguardian.com/environment/2020/mar/18/tip-of-the-iceberg-is-our-destruction-of-nature-responsible-for-covid-19-aoe

11   Food and Agriculture Organization of the United Nations, 'Key facts and findings', fao.org. http://www.fao.org/news/story/en/item/197623/icode/

12   Hannah Ritchie and Max Roser, 'Environmental impacts of food production'. ourworldindata.org. January 2020. https://ourworldindata.org/environmental-impacts-of-food

13   Greenpeace, 'Slaughtering The Amazon', https://www.greenpeace.org/usa/wp-content/uploads/legacy/Global/usa/planet3/PDFs/slaughtering-the-amazon-part-1.pdf

14   Andrew Wasley, Fiona Harvey and Madlen Davies, 'Serious farm pollution breaches rise in UK – and many go unprosecuted', theguardian.com, 21 August 2017. https://www.theguardian.com/environment/2017/aug/21/serious-farm-pollution-breaches-increase-many-go-unprosecuted

15   Greenpeace Africa, 'Ghost gear: the abandoned fishing nets haunting our oceans', 6 November 2019. https://www.greenpeace.org/africa/en/blogs/8248/ghost-gear-the-abandoned-fishing-nets-haunting-our-oceans/

16   Cordis, 'The worrying state of Mediterranean fish stocks', 3 April 2017. https://phys.org/news/2017-04-state-mediterranean-fish-stocks.html

17   Fish Forward Project, https://www.fishforward.eu/en/project/by-catch/

18   Clara Guibourg and Helen Briggs, 'Which vegan milk is best?', bbc.co,uk, 22 February 2019. https://www.bbc.com/news/science-environment-46654042

19   Briana Pobiner, 'Evidence for meat-eating by early humans', https://www.nature.com/scitable/knowledge/library/evidence-for-meat-eating-by-early-humans-103874273/

20   Hannah Ritchie, 'Which countries eat the most meat?', bbc.co.uk, 4 February 2019. https://www.bbc.com/news/health-47057341

21   Compassion in World Farming, https://www.ciwf.org.uk/factory-farming/animal-cruelty/

22   Financial Times, 'Have We Reached Peak Meat?', 26 Dec 2019, https://www.ft.com/content/815c9d62-14f4-11ea-9ee4-11f260415385

23   Guardian, 'Almost one in four food products launched in UK in 2019 labelled vegan', 17 January 2020, https://www.theguardian.com/food/2020/jan/17/almost-one-in-four-food-products-launched-in-uk-in-2019-labelled-vegan

24   PETA UK, '44 accidentally vegan snack foods', peta.org.uk, 20 January 2019. https://www.peta.org.uk/blog/44-accidentally-vegan-snack-foods/?utm_source=PETA%20UK::Google&utm_medium=Ad&utm_campaign=1217::veg::PETA%20UK::Google::grant::::searchad&gclid=CjwKCAjwi_b3BRAGEiwAemPNU4VbgGkfWgtPnyfJq7wT9rwQlqeRqNX2Kp-vNNJLYol7iMVZol9h3BoCCM8QAvD_BwE

25   Heather McClees, 'Casein: The disturbing connection between this dairy protein and your health', onegreenplanet.org, 2019. https://www.onegreenplanet.org/natural-health/casein-dairy-protein-and-your-health/

      https://www.forbes.com/sites/michaelpellmanrowland/2017/06/26/cheese-addiction/

26   One egg yolk contains around 185 milligrams of cholesterol, which is more than half of the 300mg daily amount of cholesterol that the US dietary guidelines recommended until recently) https://www.bbc.com/future/article/20190916-areeggs-good-for-you

27   Heather Russell, 'Introducing VNutrition', vegansociety.com, 30 January 2018. https://www.vegansociety.com/whats-new/blog/introducing-vnutrition

28   Hannah Ritchie and Max Roser, 'Environmental impacts of food production'. ourworldindata.org January2020. https://ourworldindata.org/environmental-impacts-of-food

29   PETA UK, 'The UK's best vegan fish and chip spots', peta.org.uk. https://www.peta.org.uk/living/vegan-fish-and-chips/

30   Euro Group For Animals, 'New report reveals toxic fur in children's clothing', 9 February 2015 https://www.eurogroupforanimals.org/news/new-report-reveals-toxic-fur-childrens-clothing

31   Save On Energy, 'Material Decomposition'. https://www.saveonenergy.com/material-decomposition31/

32   League Against Cruel Sports, https://www.league.org.uk/greyhound-racing

Notes

Awakenings

Notes

Awakenings

"

What's important is that we continue to evolve and work together to make this world a better place for us and the animals we share it with.

"

> **"**
>
> What's important is that we continue to evolve and work together to make this world a better place for us and the animals we share it with.
>
> **"**